The Dominie

The Dominie

by Walter Wingate

The Dominie is growing grey, and feth he's keepit thrang,
Wi' counts an' spellin' a' the day, an' liffies when they're wrang.
He dauners out at nine o'clock, He dauners hame at four —
Frae twal to ane to eat and smoke — And sae his day is owre!
Oh! Leezie, Leezie, fine and easy is a job like yon —
A' Saturday at gowf to play; And aye the pay gaun on!
When winter days are cauld and dark and dykes are deep wi snaw
and bairns are shiverin' owre their wark, He shuts the shop at twa,
And when it comes to Hogmanay, And fun comes roarin' ben,
And ilka dog maun tak' a day, The dominie tak's ten!
Oh! Leezie, Leezie, fine and easy is a job like yon —
To stop the mill whene'er you will, And aye the pay gaun on!
And when Inspectors gi'e a ca' He tak's them roun' to dine,
And aye the upshot o' it a' — 'The bairns are dae'in fine!'
And sae the 'Board' come smirkin' roon Wi prizes in their haun,
And syne it's free the end o' June until the Lord kens whan!
Oh! Leezie, Leezie, fine and easy Is a job like yon —
Sax weeks to jaunt and gallivant, And aye the pay gaun on!

The Dominie

A Profile of
the Scottish Headmaster

WILLIAM F. HENDRIE

JOHN DONALD PUBLISHERS LTD
EDINBURGH

© William F. Hendrie 1997

ISBN 0 85976 459 1

British Library Cataloguing in Publication Data
A catalogue record for this book is available
from the British Library.

Typesetting & prepress origination by Brinnoven, Livingston.
Printed & bound in Great Britain by Bell & Bain Ltd, Glasgow.

PREFACE

'Youngest Head in Scotland' announced a newspaper headline, when I was appointed headmaster of Torphichen Primary School in 1969. Headmaster, was however, a term seldom used in the wee West Lothian village where I took charge of my first school. To the pupils I was simply 'The Maister', while many of the older inhabitants still referred to me as 'The Dominie', as in the title of nineteenth-century Dumfriesshire writer Walter Wingate's popular poem.

My career took me on to become dominie of two other schools, Murrayfield Primary in Blackburn, the sprawling Glasgow overspill housing scheme built to serve the British Leyland Truck and Tractor Works, and finally to Linlithgow Primary, which, with its roll of 750 pupils, was the largest in Scotland. At all three and also earlier at my own former primary school, Bo'ness Public, where my first promoted teaching post was as Assistant Head, I frequently encouraged my pupils to bring history to life by undertaking projects on the origins of their own schools. As they delved into the past, I too became more and more intrigued to find out about my predecessors, the dominies, who had contributed so much to Scottish education.

Men like John Elder, who I mention in Chapter 1, one of my Victorian predecessors at Torphichen, whose weather-worn tombstone in the south wall of the kirk close by the school where he taught, states that he devoted over forty years, the entire length of his teaching career to educating the bairns of the one village and that his memorial was erected in gratitude by his former scholars.

This book is about the dominies like him, the unsung heroes and admittedly sometimes villians of Scottish education, who chiselled out lessons at the chalkface, rather than the well-known names such as A.S. Neill and R.F. MacKenzie, whose liberal theories have been written up in college textbooks and captured newspaper headlines, but did little to influence the typical school days of most Scottish pupils.

This book is dedicated to the thousands of pupils I have taught, not only at the Lindsay High School, Bathgate, where l began my teaching career, and at the four primary schools already mentioned, but also to all of the others I encountered, all be it briefly, at West Lothian Education Authority summer camps, Scottish International Youth Camps, Benmore and Lagganlia Outdoor Education Centres, and aboard the school ships *Dunera*, *Nevasa* and *Uganda*, where I held some of my most exciting classes, and especially to the boys and girls of the Glen High School, Pretoria, South Africa, who have become my adopted pupils in my retirement.

When I first visited the Glen in 1984, l was told that I was being taken to a school which was more Scottish that any school in my homeland. Since then I have discovered this to be in many ways true. Simply because of its title, taken from a local Transvaal placename, the Glen has encouraged its 980 multiracial pupils to take pride in the clans into which they are divided instead of school houses, to be proud of the thistle they wear as their badge, and of the tartan they wear as part of their uniform, and to sing lustily their school song to the tune of 'Scotland the Brave'. Much more importantly, however, its headmaster, Anthony Wilcocks and his staff have inculcated into them many of the facets traditional to Scottish education, including a love of learning, discipline and good manners, all summed up most aptly in the Glen's carefully chosen Gaelic motto, *Urram*, meaning, 'Respect with Honour'.

Perhaps this too might have been a motto which generations of Scottish dominies strived to live up to. This is their story.

W.F.H.
1997

CONTENTS

– 1 –
LITTLE HEADS ARE HOLLOW

Ram it in, cram it in, little heads are hollow,
Belt it in, strap it in, more to come tomorrow!

This traditional playground rhyme could well have been the creed of the dominies, the schoolmasters who for hundreds of years gave Scottish education a reputation second to none in the world, a world in which their pupils made their marks in government, law, medicine, science, commerce, religion and learning, in a proportion far greater than their number.

Thanks to the teaching, thorough grounding, drilling and coaching given by the dominies, bright Scottish pupils, the famous 'lads o' pairts' as they were nicknamed, no matter how poor their backgrounds, had the opportunity, unknown in other societies in earlier centuries, to rise from the humblest beginnings to achieve the highest of positions — and many of them did.

'What did you think o' the English', the exiled Scot is said to have been asked upon his return home from London? 'I've no idea', he replied, 'I only dealt with the men at the top and like me they all hailed from Scotland!'

Who then were these dominies, and how did they produce this education system, which grew to be the envy of the rest, not only of Britain, but of the world?

The name 'dominie' comes from the Latin *dominus*, meaning 'master', and this derivation reveals a great deal about these early Scottish teachers, what they taught, the influence they wielded and the way in which they educated a nation. Team 'dominie' with the Latin *discipulus*, meaning 'pupil', and the relationship between the Scottish schoolmaster and the Scottish taught is complete, because in this strictly Calvinistic northern land there was never any confusion about school days being the happiest days. They were without doubt a stern preparation for the stern adult life to come.

It was indeed that famous pillar of the Scottish Presbyterian church, John Knox himself, who issued the best-known statement on education, when, in the year 1560, his *First Book of Discipline* decreed that there should be a schoolmaster, 'able at least to teach the grammar and the Latin tongue, in every parish of any importance'.

Having laid the basis for every child to receive elementary schooling, Knox then went on to describe how able pupils should be able to progress to secondary schools 'in every notable town, in which the arts, rhetoric and the tongues should be read by sufficient masters, for whom, as well as for the poor scholars, who cannot support themselves at their letters, provision must be made'.

Finally, Knox declared that upon completion of their schooling all children should proceed to further knowledge to be acquired at the universities, or, for the less academically inclined, through an apprenticeship, or 'other profitable exercise'.

While not all of Knox's ideas were to become realities, he did undoubtedly provide the guidelines which, during the following centuries, were to ensure that Scottish boys did have the opportunity to progress from the smallest village school to university if they had the brains to warrant it, in a way completely undreamt of in any other parts of the country.

Knox's work on education, published in 1560, was particulary necessary because, until the Reformation, to which he had contributed so much, it had been the Roman Catholic Church which had been responisble for the establishment and operation of the earliest schools.

With the original Scottish schools attached to cathedrals, abbeys and monasteries and intended mainly to provide future priests for these churches, it is not surprising to find that the first dominies were themselves members of the clergy. One of the earliest known dominies of the Grammar School of Edinburgh, Master Harry Hendryson, was reminded that he was expected to be 'at high solomne festivale tymes, at high Mass and at evin' sang, with his surples upon him, within the said Abbay of Holyrood as efferis'.

In Kirkwall, the master of the Grammar School was also the chaplain at St Magnus Cathedral and he was reminded that on solemn days, and at church festivals, he was still expected to wear his surplice while in the choir. Likewise in Aberdeen during the

1550s, the master of the Grammar School, James Chalmer, had his stall and place in the choir in the parish church.

Just as the first dominies were church men, so too the subjects taught in Scotland's earliest schools were directly linked to those which priests required to know in order to perform their duties, with Latin, and in particular Latin grammar, taking pride of place. Gradually other subjects were introduced, so that by the 1550s the dominie of Aberdeen Grammar school was ordered to ensure that he instructed his pupils not only in the Latin tongue, but also 'in arithmetic, science, manners, writing and other such virtues'.

The records of Aberdeen Grammar School do in fact present us with a very full picture of life at a Scottish school before the Reformation, from classroom lessons to playground bullying and how it should be punished.

As they entered school, shortly after dawn in summer, and before daybreak in winter, the boys were ordered to bow before the statue of Christ and the Virgin Mary, and on bended knees recite the following prayer in Latin:

> I thank Thee, heavenly Father, that Thou hast willed that the past night hath been prosperous for me; and I pray that Thou wilt also be favourable to me this day, for Thy glory and the health of my soul, and Thou who art the true light , knowing no setting, sun eternal, enlivening, supporting, gladdening all things, deign to enlighten my mind, that I may never fall into any sin, but by Thy guiding arrive at life eternal. Amen. Jesus, be Thou Jesus to me; and by Thy chief spirit strengthen me.

The Aberdeen school authorities did not, however, appear to put much faith in the prayer, for while the boys were ordered to ask God to save them fom falling 'into any sin', one of the dominie's first tasks each day was to 'enter and chastise either by word or strokes the deficients' during the first lesson of the morning'. Only after he had finished punishing the boys was the master ordered to repeat the lesson himself to ensure that they had understood it. When this was finished at 9 o'clock the boys were instructed 'to make haste to breakfast'.

By 10 o'clock they had all to be back in their places ready to listen to lessons taken by the assistant masters, while the dominie himself lectured on 'Terence, Vigil or Cicero' for the final half hour of the morning, until, 'When the hour of mid-day strikes, power will be given to the boys to go to dinner'.

In the afternoon scholars were ordered to be back at their desks 'before two o'clock for hearing the class prelections. One of the assistant masters will always be present in the school and take notes of errors and mistakes made in the Latin language and of those who are less inclined to studies. And at the fourth hour of the afternoon, the boys, after the ringing of the bell, will rehearse to their tutors the work of the day.'

Depending on how soon they could satisfy the tutors that they knew their lessons the boys could then look forward to a short break before returning to the classroom for 'evening disputations frorm the fifth to the sixth hour of night: and when that is finished, they will hasten to sing prayers to God, the best the greatest'.

With such a long day it is hardly surprising to find that one of the first school rules governed how they were to leave the room — 'at the necessity of nature'. At Aberdeen Grammar School the routine was to be as follows:

They will go out in pairs with a mark or baton. It will not be lawful for anyone else to go out, unless compelled, before the return of those to whom leave of going out was first granted.

Other rules included the following:

No one shall do injury to another by word or deed; and if he who is hurt shall bear it quietly, the offender will be punished by his complaining. But if by fighting they raise strife and altercation on both sides, each will suffer; if instead of words, blows are given, he alone who inflicts blows shall suffer punishment. If they, who are more advanced in years, by sinning in the premesis will give an occasion of transgression to the younger scholars , they will be given a double punishment, because they transgressed and gave an occasion of transgressing to scholars, who otherwise had not the mind for transgressing.

The dominie was then presented with a long list of the commonest offences for which he was to make sure that his pupils were to be soundly whipped. They included:

Those not listening to what is said; Those coming late in the morning to school; Those who do not know to say their part of the text of the lesson; Those removing unnecessarily from place to place in the classroom; Those running here and there within the room; Those talking in the time of the master taking the prelections; Those returning late from breakfast or dinner; Those dragging out the time in the work of nature; Those talking in the vernacular tongue; Those who play out of the sight of the assistant masters;

and finally, just in case any possible fault might have been missed:

Those who are the authors of any mischief.

Special rules applied to behaviour in the playground. They read:

It will not be allowed to barter, nor to buy a thing from another, nor to sell what is one's own, without first consulting the master or his assistant. No-one will play by staking a book or money, or clothes or dinner; but for a stake such as leather pins or thongs, the more advanced may contend. Playing of dice is forbidden; the poor will rejoice in the playing of dice.

With all these rules to remember it might have been of some comfort to the boys to know that there were also rules for the dominie, including one that he must hear the work of at least one class other than that of the boys in his own senior form.

Another early school of which it is possible to gain a picture from the surviving records is that of Montrose, whose George Wishart, the famous Scottish martyr, was once a pupil. Another former pupil was Andrew Melville, and one of the most interesting pieces of information known about the Montrose School is that he was taught Greek when he was at it, one of the first mentions of this ancient classical language having been taught in Scotland.

All in all the Montrose school seems to have been well ahead of its time, perhaps because it was under the charge of a French teacher called Pierre de Marsiliers, whose acknowledged scholarship had led to him being specially invited to Scotland by the well-known 16th-century churchman, John Erskine.

In 1556 the curriculum which the dominies of Montrose expected their pupils to master was detailed as:

the Catechism, prayers, Scriptures, rudiments of Latin Grammar, with the vocables in Latin and in French, diverse speeches in French with the proper pronunciation, the etymology and syntax of Lillius and Linacer, Hunter's Nomenclature, Minora Colloquia of Erasmus, Eclogues of Vigil, Epistles of Horace and the Epistles of Cicero.

Senior pupils were expected to go on to study:

The Phormic of Terence, Sebastian's Grammer, exercises in composition, the Georgics of Virgil and other diverse things.

Somehow the dominie was also expected to find time to teach his pupils to 'handle the club for golf', and Andrew Melville's nephew James also states that during the years immediately after the Reformation the master taught the boys to swim, which is by far the earliest mention of either of these sports in any Scottish school.

After the Reformation the connection between churchman and dominies remained close, because many of the school masters were in fact 'Stickit' ministers, that is, divinity students who for one reason or another had not completed their course, but who eventually still hoped to occupy a pulpit.

Until the 1840s there was indeed no special training for teaching, the qualifications looked for usually being simply a master's degree or at least evidence of attendance at one of Scotland's four universities, followed perhaps by some practical experience as a doctor, or usher, or as an assistant teacher in one of the larger schools was called.

Just as today, with teachers and headmasters, dominies varied greatly in character, style, and the degree of interest which they showed for their profession. At least one, John Elder, dominie of Torphichen, near Bathgate in West Lothian, devoted the whole of his teaching career to the bairns of the one village, coming to its little stone-built single-roomed school as a young man straight from Edinburgh University, and staying there until he retired over forty years later.

On the other hand, others stayed no longer than many modern teachers in the 1990s, whose comings and goings make school staffrooms seem more like airport arrival and departure lounges.

Sometimes the 17th- and 18th-century dominies moved swiftly to larger, better-paid schools, but far more than in the present day gave up teaching either because they recognised their own problems with discipline or lessons, or quickly had them pointed out to them by the town councillors and members of the kirk session who had appointed them, often on a trial basis.

Much of what we know about the dominies of former centuries does in fact come from the details placed before the councillors, minister and kirk session members when jobs were being settled.

One of the most surprising details to emerge is the youth of many of the applicants, seventeen and eighteen being quite common, because boys entered university at a much earlier age than they do today. Having gained their masters degree they were considered eligible to become dominies without any specific training for the job.

It was not until the middle of the last century, in 1846, that the Privy Council established the first recognised training system for Scottish teachers. It was called the P.T. System. In this case P.T. had nothing to do with the 'Physical Torture' that Scottish children maintained was inflicted upon them in later years in the gymnasium, but stood for 'Pupil Teachers', boys and girls aged thirteen or fourteen who were trained within the schools themselves. 'Penny Teachers' the bairns called them, and there was a great deal of truth in this nickname because they were paid the princely sum of from £10 to £20 a year.

For many years officialdom preferred to ignore the P.T. system, as it aimed only to produce teachers for the poorest schools in the new industrial towns, while the true dominies were still university graduates. In 1910, Sir John Struthers altered it to the Junior Student System, which, while still allowing boys and girls to gain practical experience in the classroom, also encouraged them to continue their own studies and go on to university, or, in the case of the girls, to one of the new teacher training colleges.

Half a century later, as Scottish primary schools struggled to cope with the post-war baby boom, men were also finally allowed to qualify for teaching by attending these training colleges, or Colleges of Education as they were by then known.

– 2 –
THE STICKIT MEENISTERS

'Stickit Meenisters' was sometimes used as a term of contempt for dominies, because it was true that many of the students who applied for teaching positions in Scottish schools, did harbour ambitions to study further to gain their degrees in divinity and thus a place in the pulpit. Once they started teaching, however, many found it hard to find time for their own studies and stuck in the classroom for the whole of the rest of their careers.

While 'Stickit Meenisters' was undoubtedly a somewhat derogatory term, it would be wrong to assume that those who were appointed dominies were ill-qualified, because members of Scottish town councils and kirk sessions were usually very demanding as far as the academic qualifications of applicants were concerned. Not content with university degrees, they also frequently set their own examinations for prospective dominies.

Such was the case in Aberdeen in 1636 when 'All young scholars, who are fit to teach grammar and desirous to be admitted one of the doctors of the grammar school' were ordered 'to compear within the Session, to undergo trial of their learning, good life and conversation, to the effect that the best and most qualified may be admitted to office'.

Nor was the examination which the would-be dominies had to face just a formality. In Aberdeen the test lasted all of four days, during which the young aspirants had to show their abilities, not just at reading and translating the Greek and Latin classics, but also their skills in teaching, public speaking, composition in prose and the writing of poetry. In Kirkcaldy, prospective dominies were even expected to 'sing a tune of music' in front of the assembled examiners.

Even after such a thorough test, the examiners sometimes could not make up their minds. In Aberdeen, in 1602 for instance, the examiners decided two candidates so good that they declared the public examination a tie, and appointed them, 'conjunct masters of the grammar school for the instruction of the youth in the art of grammar, good letters and manners'. How the two dominies co-existed or divided their duties is unfortunately not recorded.

On other occasions, at the end of the examinations, the burgh magistrates and members of the kirk session did not consider any of the candidates fit 'to teach the bairns of the parish'. Such was the case at Forfar in 1793, when the bailies, having considered the report submitted by the local minister, decided that none of the four students was 'qualified to teach the Latin grammar and accordingly do not think it proper to admit any one of the candidates, but on account of their trouble and expense in attending the competition, they allow each of them a guinea for defraying their expenses'.

Sometimes the examiners' lack of satisfaction with would-be dominies appears to have been caused by the fact that local landowners considered the post under their patronage and put forward young men who had their ear, rather than suitable qualifications. In Dunfermline for instance, patronage of the grammar school belonged to Lord Yester, and the councillors and his lordship fell out in 1703, when they announced that the 'presentee, having them examined in the fundamentals of grammar, gave no proof of his abilities to convey a clear notion to the boys. Having also been examined in the most common pieces of Terence, Juvenal, Cicero's Orations, Livy and the Odes of Horace, he was found to be considerably defective in the reading, construction and exposition of the Latin and that he acknowledged his ignorance of mythology, Roman antiquity, Roman calendar, geography, chronology and scanning of verse, and having been put to making a theme and a version, he acquitted himself indifferently in the former and made nothing of the latter.'

Often the appointment of a new dominie resulted in tremendous quarrels in a town between the local landowners or heritors, the Provost and magistrates and the minister, and members of the kirk session, all of whom thought they knew best about who the new 'maister' ought to be.

In 1631 in Perth, the Provost and his baillies decided to simplify the whole business by not bothering even to consult the minister and his elders, when it came to appointing the new Rector for the town's grammar school. Unilaterally they appointed a Mr John Roy and made a public announcement about their decision. Furious, the minister and members of the session wrote to the magistrates stating that they were, 'offendit, because they weld have bein at palcing ane man of their ain'.

The Provost and councillors refused to give way and went ahead with Mr Roy's induction to the school. The minister and session in their turn boycotted the ceremony, and, according to Perth's burgh records, indicated that they were, 'mychtele miscontent'. The minister then, 'daylie railitt out of the pulpett aganes the Provost, Baillies and Counsall and thairefter did complene to the Preshiterie'.

The Presbytery, the local governing body of all of the presbyterian churches in the area, snubbed the Provost and council by ignoring them and summoned the new dominie to appear before it at its next meeting, to explain why he had accepted the position of Rector of Perth Grammar School without its blessing. Instead of so doing, Mr Roy went to the next meeting of the town council to seek advice about what he should answer to the Presbytery and was told to tell the ministers and elders that his appointment had absolutely nothing to do with them and that he must obey his patrons, the councillors.

In the end the whole sorry business reached its climax, when the Presbytery issued a direct challenge to the council and were informed in turn by the Provost and magistrates that, 'we refuse to acknowledge the authority of the presbiterie, except they doubt Mr Roy's qualifications'. The ministers, 'departed malcontentent', but from then on Mr Roy was left to teach in peace.

Quarrels about the appointment of dominies did not always polarise between the councillors, members of the kirk session and heritors, but equally frequently caused as much strife amongst their own members. In 1662, the burgh council of Jedburgh, 'remembering the great divisions, quarreling, controversies and debates, formerly among the inhabitants of the burgh, anent the placing and displacing of the late schoolmaster, being a division tending to the burgh's great prejudice and being now anxious that the vacant office in the grammar school shall be supplied with an able schoolmaster and that all controversy and debate may be fully extinguished and taken away, all, in one voice nominate Mr Peter Black, minister of the burgh, to give a call to a qualified schoolmaster, for whom all shall be answerable'.

In 1666, the Provost and a Bailie of Peebles were authorised to go to Edinburgh, 'to spear oot a schoolmaster'. This practice of sending a delegation to seek a suitable candidate rather than waiting for the candidates to apply for the post, was followed by many other burghs, including Stirling, which, in 1727, appointed two Bailies and the Dean of Guild to inform themesleves, 'in a prudent manner', of the 'moral character of Mr Erskine, who is recommended for the office of master of the Grammar School'.

Frequently these deputations even sat in on the applicant's lessons in his existing school, 'to tak' trial of him', or 'to try the qaulity and present condition of the maister', as it was expressed in Glasgow in 1642. On the other hand, other burghs insisted on seeing the new would-be dominie teach in their own school before confirming his appointment. In Banff in 1742, for instance, the council informed a candidate, 'That if after a trail of his conduct and behaviour for a few months, shall be satisfactory', he would receive the appointment. In 1756 a junior teacher, who was described as an usher, was not finally confirmed to his new post at the town's grammar school until after a 'trial be made of his diligence and qualifications for discharging that duty'.

When a new dominie had finally satisfied all those involved in his appointment and sworn a vow of religious observance, his installation was frequently accompanied by far greater ceremony than anything which takes place nowadays. Often the town crier or bellman accompanied by the town drummer paraded through the streets, summoning all the parents to attend the installation. As the mothers and fathers crowded the long wooden benches normally occupied by their offspring, the minister usually started the proceedings with prayers seeking the Lord's blessing on the new dominie, whose praises were then sung by the provost, followed by similar glowing descriptions from the bailies and other councillors.

Then the new dominie stepped forward and shook hands with all of the platform party, who in turn promised to support him in his work. Finally, he was presented with the keys of the school and usually with a gift. These presents varied in different parts of Scotland. In Aberdeen it always took the form of a new Latin grammar book, but further south in Perth and Cupar they appear to have taken a somewhat more practical and definitely grimmer view of life in the classroom, because in these towns they always presented their incoming dominies with 'a pair o' leather taws'.

Thus armed, the new dominie was then expected to show his prowess as a teacher by ringing the school bell, and, the children having assembled, teaching his first lesson in front of all of their parents and the waiting councillors. This ordeal over, the bairns were then dismissed for the remainder of the day and the dignitaries invited the new dominie to join them for a meal, while no doubt keeping a close eye on how much he dared to drink!

In more recent decades it has sometimes been alleged that newly appointed dominies owed their promoted posts to supplying hospitality in the opposite direction, by ensuring that members of the education committee were well entertained before the selection meeting took place. Equally entertaining are the many stories about canvassing, the reprehensible practice which expected candidates for headships to go cap and references in hand, knocking on town and county councillors' doors to attempt to persuade them that they were definitely the right man to vote for at the forthcoming selection interview.

One well-known retired dominie still vividly recalls the night when, earlier in his teaching career, he went canvassing in Stirlingshire, only to find a queue of his rivals already lining the walls of the close outside the tenement home of one of the members of the education committee. At last it came his turn to be admitted to the presence of the great man, who he found seated with his feet in a basin of water in front of his kitchen range. All the points in the dominie's favour, which he had hoped to put across went unrecited as he spent the next ten minutes listening to a liturgy of complaints about the councillor's corns and how he had acquired them walking the streets of the town, 'for to see to' the interests and complaints of his constituents. As the councillor dried his feet and his corns, the prospective dominie prepared to take his leave, but not before the councillor advised him, 'Noo, mind, if I vote for you, I expect you to mak' sure the bairns dae their grammar every day'.

When an Edinburgh dominie went canvassing for promotion to one of the city's larger primary schools, it was not his grammar, but his mental arithmetic, which he found under test, when a football coupon was pushed across the kitchen table at him. 'Just add up these lines, son, while I hae a keek at they references of yours', commanded the member of the city's education committee, before adding insult to injury by announcing, 'Ye ken, I cannae see a thing since I smashed my specs'.

During the 1950s the councillors on the Education Committee of Dundee Education Authority made a determined but abortive effort to be the first in Scotland to ban the belt from all of their city schools, so a prospective dominie was not at all surprised to be asked several questions at his interview about corporal punishment and how often and for what classroom offences it should in his opinion be used. He was however somewhat nonplussed when one councillor demanded, 'Do you think capital punishment should be used on girls?'

– 3 –
THE DOMINIE'S NOT SO HAPPY LOT

Short hours and long holidays have traditionally been the picture of 'The Dominie's Happy Lot', as portrayed by the Dumfries-shire writer Walter Wingate, whose well known poem of that title was a favourite recitation in Edwardian drawing-rooms.

For generations of earlier dominies from the middle ages until the 19th century, however, the truth was very different. They worked very long hours, as of course did their scholars. Grant in his *Burgh Schools of Scotland* states, 'It is painful to contemplate the exhausted state, mentally and bodily of poor children, who had to attend school for ten hours a day from six in the morning to six in the evening with only two hours of intermission'.

In 1867, the Royal Commission on Scottish schools found that the dominies and their pupils worked half as long again as their English counterparts. Some of this extra time was made up of classes on Saturdays, for although Wingate, who lived from 1865 to 1918, wrote the oft quoted lines 'A' Saturday at gowf to play, And aye the pay gaun on!', weekend classes, especially on Saturday mornings were still a common feature of Scottish school life until the middle of Queen Victoria's reign, and, as mentioned in another chapter, the dominies of previous centuries also had Sunday duties.

Wingate also jocularly refers to the dominie's 'Sax weeks to jaunt and gallivant'. School holidays must indeed have seemed generous in comparison with those enjoyed by other workers in his day, but these lines of his poem disguise the fact that the dominies were not free all of the time that their pupils were out of class.

For, partially because they were so poorly paid, and partially because it was expected of them, dominies for centuries had to put up with the tyranny of what was known as plurality. This meant that the dominies had many additional duties outside of school hours, and these usually continued throughout holiday periods.

Some of these originated in the 16th century, when, following the Reformation, the dominies were often amongst the few townsfolk of Scottish burghs who were truly competent at reading and writing. This meant that they were called upon to act as Session Clerk to the Kirk Session, recording all of the births, marriages and deaths in the parish. Then on Sundays the dominies were often lay readers in the kirk, and precentors, leading the unaccompanied singing of the psalms and hymns. In Ayr, for instance, in 1595 the dominie was called upon to read the prayers at the Sunday morning service and also read again, this time from the Bible, after the minister finished preaching both in the morning and the afternoon. In some burghs the dominie was also the church beadle, helping the minister don his vestments before each service, escorting him into the kirk, carrying the Bible up the steps, and placing it open and ready at the correct place in the pulpit, from which he collected it again at the close of worship.

Often the dominies' church-related duties were not confined to Sundays, but occupied time on weekdays after school hours as well. In 1703, in Banff, the council unanimously decided that their dominie should say morning and evening prayers, and give a reading from the Bible every weekday of the year. What the over-burdened dominie thought of their decision is not recorded.

As it was known that many of the dominies hoped to progress in their studies to become ministers, some of the burgh councils appear to have thought they were doing them a favour by allocating them these church duties. For instance, in Ayr, the councillors promised to use their influence to get their dominie elected as the Session Clerk of the new kirk. In 1663, the dominie of the Fife east neuk fishing port of Pittenweem is recorded as acting as 'preceptor and Session Clerk as well as doing other things incumbent on the schoolmaister'.

In 1700, in the Highland parish of Fortrose on the Black Isle, the council delivered to the dominie as Session Clerk 'the church Bible, the register of baptisms and marriages and the register of the distribution of the mortifications of the poor ones'.

In addition to church duties, dominies were often expected to be their town's Burgh Clerk, as, for instance, in Kinghorn, on the coast of Fife, in 1581. Two centuries later, in 1784, the schoolmaster in Inverurie in Aberdeenshire was appointed depute Town Clerk.

While the dominies' competence as writers may have justified the local expectancy that they would be clerks for both their towns and their churches, it was no doubt their mathematical abilities which were put to work when they were made responsible for ringing the bells, winding up the town clocks and ensuring that they kept good time. In 1592 for instance, when Mr Robert Nairn was appointed dominie in Linlithgow, his duties included tending the clock in the Town House. Sometimes, however, dominies were apparently paid extra for their clock-minding chores, because in 1731 the dominie in Ayr presented his account for 'dressing and heightening the town clock and assisting at the bells in July, the last for several days'.

The dominies' ability to do sums also meant that they were put in charge of some of Scotland's earliest savings banks. They were often also charged with collecting the dues from those who borrowed books from some of the country's earliest subscription lending libraries, before free public libraries were established in Victorian times.

On the subject of reading, some dominies, as nowadays, added to their salaries by writing textbooks. One of the earliest mentions of money being made in this way comes in 1559, when Master William Nudrye was granted a monopoly for publishing school books. In 1634, David Wedderburn, master of the Grammar School of Aberdeen, published a Latin grammar book for which the city council paid him £50. Most successful of the early Scottish schoolmasters writers of school books was Thomas Ruddiman, who, in 1714, published his *Rudiments of the Latin Tongue*, which during his lifetime ran to no fewer than 15 editions.

Another modern source of income for some teachers is working as interpreters, especially with the increase in trade with the common market countries, but this too has its historic predecent. In the Fife fishing village of Crail, in 1781, the dominie was paid by the local council for translating a document from Latin into English. The town records note that the dominie, Mr Coldstream, took 'vast trouble' over this task, and, the translation being done to the satisfaction of the councillors, they rewarded him with the princely sum of 15 shillings.

Some of the early Scottish councils even on occasion required their

dominies to try their hands at writing poetry'. When King James Vl
brought his young bride, Princess Anne of Denmark, to Edinburgh
for the first time, the royal procession was halted at the 'straight of
the Bow' while the dominie of the High School, Hercules Rollock,
read the verses which he had prepared specially for the occasion.
Later, after King Jamie survived the attempt to assassinate him at
the Gowrie Conspiracy, the councillors of Aberdeen paid dominie
Thomas Cargill, master of the city's grammar school, £20 for writing
a treatise in Latin congratulating the monarch on his escape. The
same dominie turned poet again, writing verses in Latin
congratulating Lord Marischal on erecting the city's new college, but
this time he was paid only £3.

King James Vl, after he had also become King James I of England,
was the subject of even more schoolmasterly verses when he paid
his first and only return visit to Scotland in 1617, when Alexander
Home, dominie at Dunbar was appointed orator to welcome him
home. When, on that same royal progress through Scotland, King
James reached Linlithgow, he suddenly found himself confronted by
an enormous plaster effigy of a lion. Concealed within was the royal
and ancient burgh's dominie, who bore the appropriate name of
Wiseman. As the king passed him he bellowed out the verses of the
well-known Scottish poet, William Drummond, who, as a local
resident, had been specially commissioned by the councillors to write
them. Dominie Wiseman ended with the words:

> No lion till these times his voice did raise up to such a Majesty; then
> king of men,
> The king of beasts speaks to thee from his den,
> Who though he now enclosed be in plaster
> When he was free, was Lithgow's wise schoolmaster.

Sadly, neither the reaction of King James, nor of dominie
Wiseman's pupils is noted in the burgh records, but it is intriguing
to wonder if his starring role perhaps led to a new nickname for the
schoolmaster.

Having been the many instigators of obliging their dominies to
take on all these extra duties by the 18th century, some Scottish town
councils began to object on the grounds that these other chores were

leading to the neglect of their schools. As early as 1702 the city fathers of Dundee warned their dominies 'not to exercise any trade of merchandise, which doth very much hinder their attendance on the school, on pain of dismissal'. Then in 1711, the Council of Dunfermline appointed the dominie at their grammar school, on condition that he 'doth engage in nae ither business'. Then in Ayr in 1772, things really came full circle when the council, harking back to the long held notion of the stickit minister, decreed that 'no person, who has any view towards the ministry need offer himself as candidate' for the post of dominie.

As Grant noted however, in *The Burgh Schools of Scotland*, 'If the school patrons — instead of passing acts prohibiting their teachers to engage in any business calculated to divert them from their proper duties — had placed them in easy circumstances, or even beyond the distressing cares of indigence, they would have taken the surest means to promote the virtue, usefulness and education of their children, the highest interests of the country and the welfare and happiness of the poor instructor, who having toiled at his little school for many years, could not look into the future without much uneasiness and dark forebodings. Who could in these circumstances blame the poor teacher for trying to turn an honest penny outside the profession for which he had already made so much sacrifice. It was an ill-judged economy to deal meanly with those whom we had entrusted with imparting to our children virtuous and useful education'.

– 4 –
AND AYE THE PAY GAUN ON

'Sax weeks to jaunt and gallivant, And aye the pay gaun on', read the lines in the well-known poem, 'The Dominie's Happy Lot', by Walter Wingate. But just how well paid were the school masters of past centuries ?

Exactly how much an individual dominie received is a very complicated matter to work out, because, in addition to his salary, he was also entitled to a rent-free school house, a piece of land on which to grow his own food, and all or most of the fees, which his pupils had to pay.

The latter fact meant that it was therefore of great importance to the dominie that all of the bairns of the parish attended the school, and explains why so many of the masters were very quick to take action if any so-called adventurer dared try to open a rival school anywhere in their territory. In 1698 the council of Stirling 'forbade any child above six years of age to be taught in other than the grammar school, nor shall anyone have liberty to keep a private school'.

Sometimes decrees like this caused bitter disputes with parents, especially where they did not like the dominie of the parish school or his methods, or his curriculum, or his strictness, or conversely, his lack of discipline, and therefore objected strongly to having to contribute to the payment of his salary through their children's fees. Such was the case in Peebles in 1682, when no less a person than the former provost of the town, John Govan, led a group of disgruntled parents who withdrew their sons from the grammar school and sent them instead to a private school in the burgh. In the end they were summoned to court. In their defence they pled that they would not send their children back to the grammar school 'unless there be a settled schoolmaster, which the present master, Mr MacMillan is not, being a preacher and about to get a kirk'.

Former Provost Govan and his fellow protesters lost their case and were each fined £10, but even more interesting is their allegation that the master looked upon teaching at the grammar school as only a temporary job, and, 'was about to get a kirk'. As mentioned in the earlier chapter on appointments, dominies were, indeed, often 'stickit ministers' who had failed their examinations, or for some other reason left university without satisfactorily completing their divinity courses.

Perhaps it was because so many dominies aimed ultimately to swap their Latin primer for an Old Testament, and their blackboard for a pulpit, that it was taken for granted in most parishes that they would undertake a wide variety of church chores, or it may simply have been that they were among the few people in the burgh, or village, with sufficient knowledge to read and understand the records, and to write down the details of the local hatches, matches and dispatches as the later local newspapers were to term local births, marriages and deaths. In any case, the dominies seem to have been glad to do these extra jobs as a welcome means to supplement their meagre official earnings.

Many and varied were the additional duties which dominies are recorded as being responsible for. One typical example of these extra tasks, and the supplementary income which they produced, is recorded at Mid Calder, near Livingston, in what is now West Lothian. In this small rural community the dominie's basic salary during the early part of the 19th century was £34 4s 4d and one half penny, plus £65 from his pupils' fees. Added together this gave him an annual income of just under £100, but in addition he was provided with a rent-free school house and received a payment of £1 6s 8d to make up for the lack of a garden in which to grow his food. Then he received £11 2s 2d and a half penny for teaching church music to both the children and adults in the congregation at the Kirk of Calder; £5 os od for acting as precentor, leading the unaccompanied psalm-singing in the kirk each Sunday; £8 8s od for calling the marriage banns at the morning services; £3 8s od for acting as the clerk to the kirk session and recording all of the births, marriages and deaths in the parish, as well as writing up the minutes of each session meeting; £2 2s od for being clerk to the heritors, that is, those who paid feues for their land in Mid Calder, and finally £5 os od for administering the local poor fund. Taken all together, these additional earnings raised his total income to £135 11s 3d which was almost four times the salary at which he was officially appointed.

Other ways which dominies found to boost their salaries included giving private tuition to the sons and daughters of richer parents, holding a night school for the older youths of the town who were at work during the day, or even by accommodating pupils as boarders in the school house. One village where boarders' fees were noted frequently as an additional source of income for the dominie was Dalmeny, eight miles to the west of Edinburgh on the hill behind the royal burgh of Queensferry. Dalmeny was particularly recommended for this purpose to the gentry of the city, because 'its country aspect and the sweetness of its air' was claimed to be much better for children's health than the atmosphere of Auld Reekie's Old Town, crowded as it was around the High Street with its dank, dark, evil-smelling closes which were often the source of the plague.

Other dominies earned a little extra organising 'a penny bank' before the major Scottish banks became established.

No matter what their way of earning some vital extra money however, the dominies had always to be very careful that their additional occupations outside of the classroom were 'proper and decent'. They could otherwise find themselves in trouble with both the local magistrates and members of the kirk session who were all always jealous that their schoolmaster should guard his status in their community, even if the salary they provided for him scarcely allowed him to do so. In the south-west, in Kirkcudbright for instance, the dominie was bound 'not to meddle with any other employment that may divert him from his office'.

James Grant, the author of *The Burgh and Parish Schools of Scotland*, noted in Victorian times:

> The poor schoolmaster was sure to be candidate for any office, which became vacant in the burgh...any gentile employment which contributed a little towards his maintenance; indeed, but for the emoluments derived from some of these offices, especially those which he so frequently held in connection with the church, his income was so mean, that in many cases it was hardly adequate to supply the necessaries of life.

Even finding the dominie's basic salary seems to have taxed some towns to the limits of their ingenuity. In 1663, the schoolmaster of Pittenweem, in the East Neuk of Fife, received part of his salary from fines levied by the kirk session on local delinquents and malefactors whose sins had been discovered. In 1721, the dominie of Dunbar had his salary made up of fees from baptisms and marriages, while in Dundee in 1773, the English masters' salaries were paid partly by the kirk and partly by a tax imposed on beer, a case no doubt of ale and spirits.

Sometimes salaries were paid by rich individual benefactors such as James Heriot, who in 1616 left money in his will to pay the salaries of the four masters at the High School of Edinburgh. Even more famous, of course, was another Heriot, Jingling Geordie, the goldsmith and jeweller to King James VI and I, who died without a family and left his considerable estate to found the city's famous George Heriot's School, and the other Heriot schools whose distinctive architecture and coats of arms can still be found in various parts of the capital.

One of the first places to impose local rates on its inhabitants in order to raise funds to provide for its dominie's salary was Dysart, on the shores of the River Forth near Kirkcaldy, which did so in 1600. Another early example of the levying of local rates to pay the dominie can be found in Inverurie, which did so a few years later in 1612. Local folk were, however, as reluctant to pay these rates in those days as modern householders are to pay their council tax on their properties, and in 1693 the provost and bailies of Cupar had to instruct the burgh treasurer to borrow money if the rates did not raise sufficient to pay their dominie.

Very rarely, a few burghs actually failed to pay their dominies. One was Burntisland, in Fife, where this happened in 1700. Another was Linlithgow, where, in 1707, the year of the Union of the Parliaments, the magistrates and councillors complained that the dominie's salary 'was a heavy burden'. The poor dominie was therefore summoned before them and told that the town could not afford to pay him. He was asked to accept a reduction in his salary, and when he refused he was informed that he was dismissed!

While there were, fortunately, few towns as bad as this, others did fall behind with their payments to their dominies. Such was the case with Kirkcudbright, which gave a bond to the schoolmaster as security for what remained unpaid of his salary in 1699. Later in 1745, the year of the second Jacobite Rebellion, Crail, in Fife, had to find £226 to make up back pay which it owed to its dominie.

With such uncertainty about payment of their salaries, dominies must have valued their pupils' fees, because, small though these were, they were at least paid over directly to the master himself, either every week or each term, and paid in advance. Many examples of school fees are to be seen in the *Second Statistical Account of Scotland* published during the 1840s. Typical are those for Bathgate, West Lothian, where the pupils were expected to pay two shillings each quarter for English, or three shillings each quarter for English with writing, while for a further sixpence arithmetic was included, but those who wished to study 'practical mathematics' had to pay a further five shillings, and a similar additional fee was charged for both Latin and French.

When bairns failed to pay their fees, dominies had two alternatives. They could expel the child concerned or they could seek out the parents to collect the debt. This latter choice could, however, be dangerous, as Alexander Sutherland, the dominie at Eick, in Aberdeenshire, found out to his cost in 1710. Unfortunately for him he met one of his defaulting parents as he walked up the village loan, as the common land was called. When he asked for the fees which were owed to him he received instead 'a blow upon the mouth, which loosened his tooth and the blood spued out and fell down upon his barb'.

Each year the dominies could also look forward to receiving some monetary gifts from their scholars. These presents were by custom usually handed over at Candlemas, at the beginning of February. On that date, Grant, in his *Burgh Schools*, published last century, notes that, 'The master sat at his desk, exchanging for the moment his usual authoritative look for placid civility'. As each boy and girl arrived at school they presented him with a coin. Grant goes on to record that:

the sum being generally proportioned to the abilities of the parents, sixpence and a shilling were the most common sums, but a few gave half and whole crowns, and even more. When the offering was less than the quarterly fee, little or no notice was taken of it, but when it was equal to that sum, the master shouted, 'Vitat', to twice the fee, 'floreat bis', to a higher sum, 'floreat ter', for a guinea and upwards, 'Glorieat'. The highest donner was publicly declared, 'Victor', 'King' or 'Queen'. At the conclusion of the ceremony of the presenting the free offerings, the children, being dismissed for a holiday proceeded along the streets, carrying the 'King' or 'Queen' in state.

Grant also states that dominies could look forward to receiving additional gifts from their pupils on the first Mondays of May, June and July. These gifts of money were known as bent silver, as the donations of money to the dominies took the place of the rushes known as bents, which the children had originally brought at the same times of the year to strew on the classroom floor 'to protect their clothes against the filth accumulated thereon'. The practice of the children going out to collect the reeds and rushes was discontinued because so many of the pupils were injured by the sharp hooks which were used to do the cutting on these occasions. At first, the money donations were intended to allow the dominie to purchase rushes to cover the earthen floor, but as more schools got wooden floor boards it became accepted that the money was really simply a gift for the dominie to use as he pleased.

According to Grant, however, some of the less scrupulous dominies were not content with these gifts and contrived to extort more money from their scholars by illegal means. One culprit was the master of Aberdeen Grammar School, who in 1604 was found guilty of 'taking from each bairn, on every Sunday, two pence for the poor, causing each every day in winter to furnish two candles, one being given to the master contrary to all reason; taking eight pennies each month from each scholar for bent silver; exacting from every scholar, when commencing a new book, twelve pence; causing bairns to pay silver at Candlemas for their candle, against all good order, the old custom being to take a candle but no silver'. The council ruled that, 'the weekly contribution for the poor' be discontinued, it apparently being hinted that the dominie considered himself one of the deserving, 'that each class be required to furnish only one candle each night and that scholars shall pay nothing when beginning a book but only their quarter stipend as prescribed. At Candlemas the scholars need bring two candles at pleasure, but the taking of silver in any time from any of the bairns for their Candlemas candle, (is forbidden) except from him that shall be, "King", who may give what he pleases. Two of the council shall be present in the school on Candlemas even', to see that this act be observed.'

Despite many similar local regulations, however, Candlemas gifts to the dominie continued into the 19th century, among the last recorded being at St Andrews in 1827, and as late as 1835 in Campbeltown.

One time in their careers when no doubt the dominies particularly welcomed gifts was upon their retirement, as there was no guarantee of any pensions. Whether or not a pension was granted appears to have depended entirely upon whether the members of the town council, or kirk session, thought that the dominie had served them well. Grant records that:

> In 1640 the council of Aberdeen, considering that Mr David Wedderburne, master of the grammar school, in regard of his old age and inability to serve in such a laborious and toilsome calling as the place requires, has demitted his office, in which he had faithfully served the town for forty years, and also considering that the poor master is likewise burdened with a wife and children, grant him a pension of two hundred merks yearly during all the days of his lifetime, with the condition that if they find out any other means equal to the pension, he will accept the second provision and demit the pension.

Frequently, towns opted out of paying their retiring dominie any gratuity or pension by making his successor responsible for supporting the old man. This meant that the new dominie had to use part of his salary to support his old predecessor. In 1799, for instance, in Dundee, the city council appointed a new English master for the grammar school on condition that he made a yearly payment of £15 to his predecessor.

The widows of dominies had even less security, having to appeal to the local council in the hope of receiving some help. Such was the case in 1600 when the widow and family of the late Hercules Rollock, former master of Edinburgh High School, petitioned the city fathers for assistance. Their reply read as follows:

The good town owes him nothing, but because he was their common servant and being desirous to give all others in the like rank occasion to do their duty, ordains five hundred merks to be paid out of the common good.

Fortunate indeed are today's dominies, who know that after forty years of teaching they can retire on half salary, with the opportunity if they prefer of early retirement at a younger age on proportionately lower pension, while pensions for their widows are guaranteed.

– 5 –
AT THE CHALK FACE

In many schools the desks are good and arranged according to the parallel system. One common defect is the want of a shelf below for the books and other property of the pupils and a groove for slates. This want gives an untidy appearance to the school, from the desks being littered with books, bags and slates and is seen in many schools. The expense would be small and the result in tidiness, order and moral habit, very great.

Thus wrote H.M. Inspector, Mr William Jolly, about the Church of Scotland's schools in Banff, Moray, Nairn, Inverness, Ross, Cromarty, Sutherland and Caithness in 1872. Mr Jolly appears to have been fortunate in the classrooms which he visited if this was his only cause for complaint, because many dominies do not appear to have been nearly as fortunate in the standard of accommodation and equipment in the schools where they taught.

Conditions at the chalk face in many Scottish schools do in fact appear to have been spartan according to the Burgh School Commissioners' report for 1868. In it the Commissioners divided the fifty-four burgh schools which they had visited into four categories; good, fair, indifferent and bad. Of the five which they deemed bad they wrote:

Two of the schools are absolutely unfit for human habitation in any shape. In one of them the door is hardly five feet high; the roof is thatched; there are two windows built in the front of the building, one of which is about one foot square and the other hardly two feet. In the roof are two holes to allow the smoke to escape, the fires being in the middle of the room on the floor. In the windows there is very little if any glass and on the one side of the roof there was a hole, which created a draught for ventilation. The furniture consisted of an old chair, which the master used, a desk and a few boards put around the walls for the children to sit on. The master lives 'but and ben' with the school and his part of the dwelling is not much better than the scholars'. In this place there were educated twenty-nine children huddled together, poorly clad and apparently poorly educated. The master is a youth. He has a salary of £10 and the house to live in.

In another parish sixty-one children were packed together, standing, sitting or lying on the floor, so that we actually had almost to walk over them in a dark building thirty feet by fifteen feet and seven feet high, built of clay with a thatched roof, full of holes, through which the rain was pouring in upon the floor and on the children. There were two very small windows on one side and a large open hole on the other to let in a little light and air. The schoolmaster, an intelligent but sickly looking young man, complained that the building was killing him and that he would have to give up teaching unless something could be done for the school. It has been twenty years in existence and on a low average there have been fifty children each year in attendance, so that upwards of one thousand children have spent the early years of their life in this hovel in pursuit of education.

Often it did not require an official inspection to reveal deficiencies in the classroom and its furnishings. As early as 1538 the dominie of Linlithgow Grammar School complained that both he and his pupils had to 'sit on cauld stanes'. A century later it appears that the conditions in the Linlithgow school were little better because the master records that his pupils were often distracted from the lessons which he was trying to teach them by the large black beetles which frequently crawled across their desks, and which they took great delight in killing by crushing them with the heavy board covers of their Ruddiman's *Latin Grammar* books.

At least the Linlithgow laddies had desks upon which to write, which was more than their counterparts at St Andrews Grammar School had almost a hundred years later in 1725, when the dominie complained officially to the town council that 'they are necessitate to wreatt upon the floor, lying upon their bellies'. After much deliberation the councillors decided that seats should be provided but that they could not afford the luxury of desks.

In 1770 the master of the Grammar School of Forfar prayed the town council to redress

a great grievance, that all branches of learning, English, arithmetic, Latin and writing are taught in one apartment and at the same time. The inconveniences hence arising are obvious. there is great confusion and indiscriminate reading aloud, which greatly impede the scholars' progress and deprive their parents and the masters of the pleasure and the scholars of the advantage of a more orderly method. The present apartment is so confined that several boys have been dismissed for want of room, which is a lamentable reason. If these boys had received education, perhaps they might have turned out valuable members of society, but by the denial thereof, must remain like a diamond buried in the ground, unpolished by the hands of an artist.

During the 1800s many Scottish towns received fine new schools thanks to the gifts of local benefactors. These included the Nicolson Institute in Stornoway, the Anderson High School, St Andrews in Lerwick, Madras College in St Andrew's, the Bell Baxter Institute in nearby Cupar, Milne's in Fochabers, the Anderson Academy in Bo'ness, and the John Neilson Institute in Paisley.

In Bathgate it was John Newland, who had emigrated from the West Lothian town and never returned, who left the fortune which he made as a slave plantation owner in the West Indies, to build a secondary school 'to provide free education for all the bairns of my native burgh'. Thus while many Scottish children may often over the years have felt that their school days were synonymous with slavery, the boys and girls of Bathgate could actually claim a direct link.

To begin with however, it seemed very doubtful if any of Bathgate's bairns would benefit from Newland's legacy, because several of his Scottish relatives challenged his will and in the end the town received less than a quarter of the original £60,000. Even when the court's decision was announced in Edinburgh in 1815 the way was not clear immediately for the trustees, whom Newland had carefully appointed, to erect the school as he had ordered in his will, for he had also instructed that only the interest which his money accumulated was to be used, and not the capital.

At last however, by 1831, over £2,500 was available and the trustees, led by Alexander Marjoribanks, approved plans for the new Academy, which was to be built on a fine site on the hillside among the open fields to the back of the town.

The opening of the new Academy, with its classical design, its Grecian columns and its decorative urns, caused a great stir in Bathgate, for until then all the education in the town had been carried on in a number of small rooms, none of which had, of course, been specially designed for the purpose. The Academy was very different and strange from any of these one roomed establishments. It even had two floors and the boys and girls would, at times, obviously have to move from room to room. Rules would obviously be required, so an impressive list of regulations was drawn up in time for the opening day. From it the first pupils discovered that besides the customary terrors of pandies from the long thick leather tawse, they could also be fined if they dared to slide down the iron banister which wound invitingly down from the upper classrooms, or were so venturesome as to climb out onto the school roof. Even if they so much as pushed a schoolmate on the stone stairs they were warned that their Saturday penny would be in danger of confiscation.

Newland's dream of free education for every single child in his hometown was not immediately realised because the trustees, left to work with only a fraction of the capital which their benefactor had originally intended, were forced to charge fees. These ranged from 2/6 if a child was only to be taught English, to 7/6 for instruction in Latin, French, Mathematics and all other subjects which the original staff of four, including the rector, could provide for their 400 pupils.

Even classes of 100 would have proved a challenge, but during the school's early years the division of 400 boys and girls was not so equitable, with the rector teaching a comparatively small class of seniors while the youngest of the assistant masters had to cope with no less than 140 first-formers. It must say something for his discipline when parents complained that on one occasion he read a newspaper in class, while on another he even managed to fall asleep at his desk.

The Bathgate parents were never slow to complain about any laxity, real or imaginary, at their new Academy. During the 1840s every Friday afternoon was regarded as an open day for mothers and fathers to come to the school to inspect the work of teacher and child alike, and make certain that they were obtaining value for their fees. Amongst their recorded complaints are criticisms that the rector was neglecting both his French and geography lessons.

Complaints about pupils not working hard enough certainly do not seem justified, for the rector even composed a special chant made up of the multiplication tables which the children were made to sing as they changed classes, so that not a moment of the working day would be wasted.

To begin with, no special provision was made for girls, but during the 1840s a sewing mistress was appointed. She did not last long, however, because it was discovered by the trustees that the extra fees did not cover her salary, and so she was dismissed. Unfortunately this decision cost the trustees even more fees, because some of the parents removed their daughters from the Academy and sent them instead to the town's newly opened Establishment for Young Ladies.

The rival establishment was, however, short-lived. When the girls returned to the Academy the trustees reintroduced sewing lessons.

In 1869 the school was completely reorganised. The older members of staff, one of whom was over 80, were asked to resign, and those who remained now taught not one subject to all grades of pupils, but general subjects to a class in a similar fashion to that adopted in modern primary schools.

Five years later Bathgate Academy, like many other Scottish schools, received its first government grant. But it was not until 1889 that all school fees were finally abolished and John Newland's wishes fully realised.

Today Bathgate Academy is situated in modern new buildings on the edge of town, but its pupils still remember their founder once each year when, on the first Saturday in June, they take part in the John Newland's Parade.

Apart from high days and holidays the school year for both pupils and dominies was pretty monotonous unless interrupted by bad weather. Half-day holidays for snow, for instance, were much more common in the past than they are nowadays. Many pupils recall glancing hopefully out of classroom windows as snow fell and praying that it would continue unabated until lunchtime, in the hope that the dominie, worried about them getting home safely, would close the school early, giving them the afternoon off — officially to shelter at home, but unofficially to enjoy snowballing and sledging down the neighbouring hills.

Walter Wingate mentions just such an occasion in his poem, but the winter within recent memory with most unscheduled closures because of adverse weather was undoubtedly that of 1947. This almost legendary big freeze is described as follows in the log-book of one school in Central Scotland.

> 27th January. Snow has fallen heavily during the night and is still falling. 3rd February. Snow has been falling all week. Roads are very bad. The school has been carried on all week by only four teachers. A double attendance was marked and pupils dismissed and sent home at 1 p.m.

The snow just fell and fell, continuing all month until, on 26 February, the dominie wrote, 'A stormy day. Blizzard conditions. School closed at 1 p.m.' And still the snow continued to fall right into March. Almost two weeks later the entry in the log-book for 13 March reads:

> The worst blizzard for fifty years is blowing. Both roads into the village are blocked by drifts from four to ten feet deep. All pupils told to stay at home. School closed.

The school and hundreds of others across Scotland remained shut for several days, and it was the beginning of April before all of the snow finally melted and disappeared.

For the dominies the coming of spring was heralded not so much by the occasional bunch of yellow daffodils brought for his desk by one of his girl favourites, or even by a jelly jar full of tiny squirming black tadpoles borne by one of the boys as a smelly addition to the classroom nature table, but by the postie arriving with a sizeable buff-coloured official envelope stuffed full of Qualifying Examination Papers. Scottish schools never had the Eleven Plus Examination, but instead they had the much dreaded 'Qualy'. The 'Qualy' took its name from the fact that this one day of concentrated tests decided which of the dominies' twelve-year-old pupils were sufficiently bright and intelligent to qualify for a place in the senior secondary schools and in particular the 'A' classes, and which should be condemned to remain in the supplementary classes of the primary school, or the senior division, as they were sometimes known, or in later decades proceed on to junior secondary schools. Although junior secondary schools often offered excellent and very appropriate practical teaching they were branded as failures.

On the eve of the 'Qualy', dominies were allowed to give their pupils a short practice paper, and to warn them of the consequences of failing on the morrow to ensure they arrived with two carefully sharpened pencils. On the big day of the actual examination the dominies were banished from their classrooms and were replaced by outside invigilators, often the local minister and his wife, who, at the precise given time, issued the printed examination papers and then proceeded to distract the pupils by pacing endlessly up and down the aisles between the well-spaced desks, announcing at fifteen minute intervals that the time was slipping away and how much time remained.

In the early 1950s one dominie in West Lothian made the mistake of using one of the actual Qualifying papers instead of the practice one on the day before the test. The result of this mistake was that every pupil in the county had to re-sit the whole examination with fresh questions several weeks later, and there was a suspense-ridden delay before they were informed which secondary courses they were to follow.

In Scottish secondary schools spring was also always an equally stressful time as fifth- and sixth-year pupils sat their 'Highers', and dominies prayed that the seeds of learning which they had sown would be rewarded with a crop of good university entrance results which would please both the pupils' parents and the dominies' masters on the local school boards. The Scottish Higher Leaving Certificate Examination was first introduced in 1888, and despite threats to reform it, it continues to be the bench mark for success in schools throughout the whole of Scotland, something that schools in other parts of the United Kingdom with their various competing examination boards have never been able to achieve.

While spring in Scottish schools was always marked as being the examination season, autumn was, until the 1960s, the 'tattie howkin' time.

The October 'tattie holidays' were granted especially to enable pupils to leave their desks and earn a little money helping local farmers ensure that all of the potato harvest was safely gathered in before the winter frosts. The dominies had varied views on this interruption to normal classroom routine, some actively encouraging certain pupils to quit their desks for a week in the fields, while others frowned on the whole business as a disgraceful exploitation of cheap child labour.

In the late 1940s in the years following the end of the Second World War, Scottish pupils were also encouraged to go out round the hedgerows gathering pounds and pounds of bright red rose hips, but this was always done during the evenings and at weekends. The following morning, however, it was the dominie's task to weigh all of the hips which were then sent off to manufacturers who turned them into supposedly very health-giving rose hip syrup, the school and the pupils sharing equally in the money thus raised.

From the early 1940s onward Scottish dominies were well used to counting money because it was expected that, in addition to all of their other work, they would start the week at nine o'clock on Monday morning by collecting pupils' dinner money to pay for the hot lunches introduced as a wartime measure to try to ensure that children did not suffer because of rationing and continued to be well-fed and received a nourishing well-balanced diet. By this period, dominies were also expected to collect children's weekly pennies to help school funds, while on another morning later in the week the classroom was converted into a bank so that pupils could be encouraged to help the war effort by depositing their national savings money.

One thing which always came free was the mid-morning third-of-a-pint glass bottle of milk, whose contents, whether pupils wanted it or not, dominies were expected to ensure were consumed before playtime. As often as not the pupils did not at all want the milk, because in summer it arrived luke-warm and already turning sour, while in winter it was frozen and had to be thawed out by placing it next to the hot-water heating pipes around the room.

Opening the milk bottles before the morning interval was also a dangerous business as dominies uttered threats to any pupils who pushed down so hard on the cardboard tops that the contents fountained out over their classmates. Also, having to ask for a second wax-coated paper straw was definitely regarded as a heinous classroom sin. Once opened, the cardboard milk bottle tops with their small round holes in the centre had then to be saved, gathered in and dried on the hot-water radiators in the classroom, so that they could later be utilised, at handwork time for the production of woollen pompoms which were in turn used to create countless brown woolly owls at Halloween, and even more fat, round, white snowmen at Christmas.

It is interesting to ponder what the dominies of earlier centuries would have thought if told that their twentieth-century successors would be classroom milkmen, bankers and restaurant managers swapping their lunch hour for a free meal!

– 6 –
THE FOUR Rs

According to tradition, the education provided by Scottish dominies was firmly rooted in the three Rs, 'reading, 'riting and 'rithmetic', but to be accurate the term should be changed to the four Rs, because religious education was also always considered part of the basic school curriculum.

While all of the early Scottish grammar schools taught in Latin, it was expected that boys entering them at about the age of nine would be already proficient in reading and writing English. In 1598, parents seeking admission for their sons into the High School of Edinburgh were informed that 'No scholar shall be admitted who cannot read English and does not know writing'.

Boys learned to read using what were described as horn books, small wooden handled boards, which began with the first letters of the alphabet, before introducing simple words through a phonetic approach. This tradition that bairns must learn their letters has served Scottish education well, and, thankfully, teachers refused to abandon it when urged to do so in the 1960s and 70s by trendy college-of-education lecturers, promotion-seeking local authority advisers, and, sadly, even ill-informed inspectors who wanted to jump on the bandwagon of the new-fangled look-and-say method, and the even more disastrous Initial Teaching Alphabet methods. Fortunately, the teachers in the classroom mostly remained faithful to the old Scottish approach, by which they had themselves been taught, and today Scottish reading schemes based on phonics are used world-wide, some even being re-imported from the 'Scotland of the South Seas', New Zealand, whose education system owes so much to the old country.

The big attraction of the 'look and learn' reading systems of the swinging 60s and 70s was that they were supposed to be so much easier, allowing pupils to recognise even large and complicated words without having to understand their composition. The dominies of old never claimed that learning to read and write was easy, but recognised that with application and repetition boys could achieve a firm foundation upon which to build their future studies.

Hearing the boys read was considered an important daily task for the dominie, but just how difficult a one is illustrated by an approach in November 1762 from the master to the council in Ayr, pointing out that his scholars were not as proficient as he would wish because he had almost eighty of them to listen to each day. Such numbers led inevitably to such methods as reading round the class, with the temptation for the more able to read ahead despite the risk of a smack with the strap for any who dared loose the place when it eventually came to their turn.

Spelling was also a regular daily chore with again the danger of strokes of the tawse for those who either failed do their homework, or failed to remember the rules such as 'i before e except after c'. Even more dangerous was the weekly dictation exercise in which all of the words supposedly learned that week were linked together in a continuous prose passage, which was all supposed to be spelt correctly on pain of a pandie to impress on the palm each and every word which the brain had forgotten.

Learning to write could also be a painful business, as perfection in the production and presentation of copperplate was the dominies' expectation of pupils who would require this skill in their future careers where mistakes in lengthy handwritten documents were not tolerable. Dominies therefore considered it their duty to chastise any scholars who blotted their copy book, while ensuring that they, as the teachers, never erred by ensuring that they had the advantages of valved ink wells, which never spilled, and rounded rulers, which made it much easier for them to rule straight lines without the risk of a tell tale stain.

As if writing periods were not dangerous enough, many pupils took added risks by dipping tiny pieces of blotting paper in ink wells and flicking ink pellets at their rivals or enemies. Once co-education introduced the distraction of the fair sex to Scottish classrooms there was the even greater temptation to dip the ends of the girls plaits or pigtails in the ink wells, and many a laddie has gone home with redden palms for the satisfaction of seeing one of the lassies end the day with blue ends to her fair, brunette, or mousey locks.

Before going on to pen, ink and paper, dominies instructed their younger pupils in the art of writing on slates. The screech of slate pencils was a familiar noise in Scottish classrooms until even after the Second World War, when wooden framed slates were reintroduced in the 1940s as a way of saving strictly rationed paper. In some ways using slates was even more dangerous for pupils than using ink and paper, because once both sides of the slate were filled with work they had to be cleaned and this involved calculated risks. To wipe the slate clean, dominies demanded pupils bring a small wet rag in a wee air-tight tin, but while most girls complied, many boys preferred to take the risk of cleaning their slates with the cuffs of their shirts, or, even worse, committing the ultimate classroom sin of spitting on them. While there is no Scottish equivalent of the slate smashing scene in the Canadian children's classic *Anne of Green Gables*, there are certainly still lots of Scottish pupils with painful finger-tingling memories of the results of misusing classroom slates.

Slates were also frequently used at the start of learning the third R, 'rithmetic, but dominies often believed that much work in mathematics should be done orally, leading to the daily round of mental sums. One West Lothian pupil remembers his dominie's impersonation of a machine gun as he fired mental problems at the class, forbidding any pupil to sit down until answering three brain teasers correctly, and woe betide any who resorted to fingers for help. For the most part the teaching of arithmetic depended on rote learning, and the sound of the chanting of multiplication tables was the theme tune of many Scottish primary classrooms.

Arithmetic was, of course, much trickier to master before the introduction of decimalisation and metrication during the 1970s. For centuries and decades before that pupils had to cope with the intricacies of adding up columns upon columns of pounds, shillings and pence, or LSD as they were known. Pupils at Bo'ness Public School even nicknamed their dominie LSD, Lang Skinny Dunlop. The author, a pupil at this same school which overlooks the River Forth, well remembers being strapped by his qualifying class teacher for being one farthing out in a long and complicated money sum, and being told as the tawse came smacking down that it was as careless to make a mistake in a fraction as it was in a pound.

Once past the dreaded qualifying examination and on to secondary school, simple arithmetic multiplied into the horrors of algebra, where equations never seemed to be equally balanced, and geometry, where dominies expected whole theorems to be painstakingly learned. Few Scottish pupils dared forget that 'The square on the hypotenuse of a right angled triangle is equal to the sum of the squares on the other two sides', despite the fact that they never made any use of the information.

The need for dominies to impart a body of information was strengthened by the Revised Code of 1862 by which the government of the day, trying to raise standards in Scottish schools, introduced the idea of payment by results, based on good attendance and subject proficiency. Many of the best dominies bitterly regretted this, as the system meant that they now had to concentrate on teaching the basics, which could be easily tested, at the expense of more creative teaching.

Payment by results was even more firmly imposed by the Scottish Education Act of 1872, but at least one dominie determinedly found a way to escape the educational strait-jacket. He was Christopher Dawson, the dominie of Abercorn, on the Hopetoun Estate, between Queensferry and Blackness on the shores of the Forth in West Lothian. Dominie Dawson was appointed to Abercorn from his first teaching position across the river in Cupar in Fife and stayed for the whole of his remaining forty-five years as a teacher. From the time that he came to Abercorn as a young man Dawson surprised the estate workers, because instead of teaching their offspring in the crowded, cramped, dark, damp little school room, which can still be seen between the manse and the kirk, as his predecessors had laboriously done, he led them forth, Pied Piper-like about the beautiful estate, teaching as he went. The children were all encouraged on these nature walks to pick up items of interest, and, back in the classroom, Dominie Dawson caused even more consternation by allowing them to push aside the wooden benches and use their desks to display their finds.

As Dominie Dawson's unusual methods became well known, regular visitors to Hopetoun House, the Marquis of Linlithgow's stately home, were persuaded to bring back exotic items from their world-wide travels, which he in turn used as object lessons for his Scottish pupils. After school too, Dawson was ahead of his time, organising extra-curricular activities for the boys and girls in his class; from swimming expeditions to the Forth at the little beach at the nearby hamlet of Society, to fishing trips.

Dawson's informal approach did not, however, mean that the Abercorn bairns lacked discipline, because they knew that the dominie could ply his tawse as capably as he wielded his trout rod. 'Be careful to check the smallest acts of disobedience and you will never be troubled with any great ones', he wrote, but while at first he was quite prepared to strap his new pupils into shape, he eventually abolished corporal punishment in a manner which again showed his individuality. In her biography of her uncle, his niece, Jean Butler, writes:

> One day in school an interesting and amusing ceremony took place. The faithful tawse, which had proved such a useful ally during the first few months, were declared to have served their purpose and outlived their usefulness and were solemnly cut in pieces, some of the girls carrying away the bits as trophies of a bygone age.

Any doubts which parents might have felt about their children's dominie's unusual approaches to lessons and discipline, so very different from the strict formal methods of neighbouring masters, were dispelled, when the Abercorn parish minister and all the members of his kirk session paid their annual visitation to the school and announced themselves completely satisfied with the pupils' progress.

Dominie Dawson's freedom to teach in his own way was however threatened, when the new Scotch Education Department in far-away London in 1872 tried to standardise Scottish educational standards by introducing its scheme for payments by results. Many of the old-style dominies decided to resign and accept the new government pensions which they were offered rather than try to adapt to the new regime, including inspections by intimidating inspectors, but Dawson, despite complaining that 'it is now expected that children shall be regularly turned out by the gross like so many little human vessels duly warranted to contain a certain amount of knowledge', decided to remain in office.

Despite complaining that he had been 'reduced to nothing more than a grant earning machine', he still managed to teach in his own fashion, while at the same time doing the Scotch Education Department's bidding, by opening the school an hour early every morning to leave time for his own curriculum approaches, without endangering his pupils' chances of passing the official tests. His scheming paid off, because in the first official inspection of Abercorn School, he was granted 'the highest possible grant for discipline and organisation'. He was also rewarded soon afterwards by the building of the fine new grey stone Gothic-style school building at White Quarries, which can be seen to the right from the M9 motorway shortly before the Linlithgow and Bo'ness Junction.

Shortly after it was built in 1878, Dominie Dawson was inundated with pupils because of the opening of a shale mine next to the new school, and the arrival of all of the miners' families. These rough tough youngsters were a new challenge for the now elderly Dawson, but he met it just as he did many others, including the education of a little Turkish boy, who was a guest at Hopetoun House and whose arrival he used as the basis for a geography lesson. Dawson continued to teach in the new school at White Quarries for over twenty years until he finally hung up his gown on 11 September 1899.

While Dawson's pioneering lessons at Abercorn School encompassed nature study, science, history and geography, the report of the Royal Commissioners in 1868 complained that the average teaching of the latter two subjects in Scottish schools was only average. It continues:

> Physical geography is taught in a very elementary way, the scholars being rarely taught the physical nature of their own country or the effects of the physical condition of a country upon its history or its people.

In Grant's *The Burgh Schools of Scotland*, published in 1876, he, very far-sightedly, recommends that 'History and geography are so nearly related that they should be taught if possible, by the same master'. Perhaps we could still belatedly heed his advice instead of perpetuating the division, which continues to damage the teaching of these subjects in Scottish secondary schools.

Grant will also be seen by many as being well ahead of his time in arguing in favour of schools, especially those in the Highlands, teaching pupils Gaelic, but dominies did not heed this advice as they felt learning English was essential to ensure their pupils' progress in their future careers. There are indeed records of dominies chastising scholars who dared to ignore the rule to speak English in the classroom, and even of Gaelic-speaking boys and girls being strapped after being overheard speaking their native tongue in the playground.

On the other hand, the Auld Alliance between Scotland and France ensured that French was taught from before the time of the Reformation. An early mention occurs in the records of Haddington for the year 1731, and another in Stirling in 1755. On the other hand, the council in Ayr in 1761 ruled that French must not be taught in the town's schools during the time allocated for Latin, Greek and mathematics and that pupils wishing to learn French must do so during the interval between school hours. There are no details of how many children were so diligent as to accept this unattractive offer or whether any parents were sufficiently Franchophiles to insist on their bairns doing so.

German was also taught in many Scottish schools, but Italian was hardly taught at all. It was mentioned only three times in the curriculum returns to the Royal Commission on Education in 1868, being taught at Tain Academy, at Websters Institute, Forfar, and at Dollar Academy where there were only six pupils studying it. In the Report of the Board of Education for 1874 it is also mentioned as being available at Perth Academy, but was being taken by only four pupils.

The marked lack of interest in Italian was in marked contrast to the days in earlier centuries when Latin was the most important subject in every Scottish grammar school, but whether its neglect was a result of its association with the Roman Church and 'Popery' is not clear, as, on the other hand, classical Latin did continue to be taught to all of the brighter pupils.

Another connection with the curriculum of Scottish schools both before and after the Reformation was religious education. It continued to occupy an important place in the teaching of all schools and still does to this day. The most recent Five to Fourteen programme recommends that a tenth of the school week during the primary and first two secondary years, that is two and a half hours, be faithfully devoted to R.E.

In his *Burgh Schools of Scotland,* Grant states:

> From the first Act passed on the subject of religious instruction by the Scottish Parliament, it appears that our forefathers were of opinion that mere knowledge is worse than ignorance — that knowledge unsanctified was not a blessing, but a curse. In 1567 Parliament asserts that all laws and constitutions provide that the youth be brought up and instructed in the fear of God and in 'gude maneris'; and declares that if God's Word be not rooted in them, their instruction shall be 'tinscil baith to their bodyis and saulis'.

In 1597 the Scottish Assembly ordained that lessons upon the catechism and grounds of religion be printed, thinking them very necessary for scholars, and in 1616 it was decreed that all pupils must be made to learn by heart the catechism. From then on memorising the catechism, even when the shorter version was acceptable, resulted in more pain than any other aspect of the school curriculum.

As late as 1800 pupils in Aberdeen spent the whole of every Saturday morning session at school painstakingly committing the shorter catechism to memory, and, just in case they forgot what they had just learned, it was specifically laid down that the new school week commence each Monday morning with them being tested in it, with strokes from the tawse for any who made mistakes.

From the Reformation until the start of the 19th century many dominies were even expected to accompany their pupils to church on Sundays and supervise their behaviour in the pews. In 1597 the Presbytery of Glasgow ordered compulsory attendance at the Cathedral, decreeing that, 'the bairns in the grammar school — all and everyone of them — shall resort to the high kirk on the Sunday to hear God's word preached and the sacraments ministered'. Again in 1685, it ordained that, 'the scholars shall convene in the school, from which they shall proceed to the church in order, with their masters. forenoon and afternoon'. In 1649 the masters and scholars attending the town's grammar school were ordered to march to church 'at the second bell in the morning and the afternoon in comely order with the masters before and to return to the school in the same order'. That same year in Peebles, the dominie was instructed to accompany 'his scholars to church when the second bell rings in the morning and afternoon in comely and decent order, noting in the time of preaching any disorder and censuring disturbers'. Likewise, in 1656 the council in Jedburgh ordered their dominie to go with his scholars to church every Sunday both in the morning and afternoon and that 'he shall be careful lest any be absent or go out of church, or spend their time idly while in church and that they shall listen reverently, account being taken of their conduct in the afternoon, when the sermon is ended'.

In 1700, the council in Aberdeen ordered that pupils should 'be called to severe account' on the Monday morning and that the dominies must chastise any who had left the church without permission or had 'caused any disturbance'. Even as late as 1826 the Aberdeen councillors insisted that 'at least one of the masters of the grammar school be present each Sunday to make provision for those scholars whose parents wish them to attend church and that they shall walk in procession to church, where the rector is to take his seat first'.

In Aberdeen the rector, the masters and the pupils were all seated together in the Grammar School Gallery. Other towns which made special provision in their churches for the dominie and his scholars included Dumbarton, Dunfermline, Kinghorn and Stirling. Dominies were also expected, in several towns, to prepare their pupils to take an active part in the acts of worship which they attended. In Dunfermline, for instance, Thomas Walker, the master of the Grammar School, was instructed 'to have his scholars ready to repeat the catechism every Sabbath betwixt the second and third bell before noon and afternoon, one proposing and the other answering, so that the people may hear and learn'. In 1700, the councillors in Aberdeen decreed that two scholars from the Grammar School should go to the city's two churches every Sunday at the beginning of the second bell in the afternoon and between the ringing of the bell and the last bell repeat such portion of the shorter catechism as had been laid down for them. In 1724 two pupils from Dumfries Grammar School were chosen, every Sunday, to repeat or read the longer or shorter catechism in the church during the time between the services to any members of the congregation who chose to remain seated in the pews.

The great emphasis upon the rote learning of the catechism appears to have typified much of the religious education in Scottish schools, with much less stress upon whether the pupils understood anything of what they were committing to heart!

It was not until the Scottish Education Act of 1872 that what was described as a 'conscience clause' gave parents the right to opt their children out of religious education classes, and, writing four years later in 1876, Grant notes that what he describes as 'this privilege' had been exercised on behalf of pupils attending Annan Academy, Arbroath High School, Ayr Academy, Edinburgh High School, Forres Academy and Hamilton Academy'.

Interestingly, Grant adds:

Teachers find it not quite easy to teach history without reference to religion, for instance, where the class-book speaks strongly against Roman Catholics; but in such cases, masters of considerate feelings, knowing that they have Roman Catholics in their class, teach the facts without comments.

Grant also refers to the fact that by the middle of the 1870s there were some ratepayers objecting strongly:

to any part of the rates exacted from them for public education being spent on the provision of religious instruction in the schools under the management of the (new) boards. These persons maintain that the public schools should be purely secular, but it may be answered that the school board elections have proved that the religious convictions of an overwhelming majority of the people everywhere would have been disregarded for the few cases in which consciences might have been relieved by establishing secular education. If the day should come when secular education will be the universal rule, knowledge may be increased, but the result we fear may disappoint the advocates of secular education.

In support of his argument, Grant then quotes the lines, 'Religion crowns the statesman and the man, sole source of public and of private peace'. He received support from the headmaster of George Watson's College, who, in the Report for Endowed Schools for 1873, stated that of his 1160 pupils all but a dozen received religious instruction and that he thought it 'necessary not only for the forming of their character, but maintaining the discipline of the school'.

While Scottish schools from the earliest time placed great emphasis on what they considered healthy minds, the idea of healthy bodies came much later, and, even in 1876, Grant wrote that:

> Gymnastics or athletic exercises have hardly yet been honoured with a place among the subjects of instruction given at our schools. Muscular exercises, being so well fitted to promote the health, strength and activity of the body, as well as order and physical obedience, should be made imperative at all schools. The different classes ought regularly to be drilled in fencing or gymnastic exercises and motions, according to the age and strength of the pupils, including marching, running, jumping, climbing, lifting and carrying, pulling and pushing. At present gymnastics are only recognised as a branch of education at two of our burgh schools — Edinburgh High School, where the class consisted in 1874 of nineteen scholars only, and Glasgow High School, where there were 195 scholars who paid a fee of five shillings to ten shillings and six pence. School boards should set apart a certain time for these exercises, and if the janitor happens to be an old soldier, he might prove a valuable addition to the staff of teachers by drilling the pupils in military exercises.

Fifty years later, the first World War provided many Scottish schools with just such a 'jannie' and many dominies appear to have been only too delighted to entrust them with the physical training of their classes. It is perhaps not surprising that pupils soon nicknamed P.T. 'physical torture', because with this teaching duty many dominies also appear to have conferred on their janitors a disciplinary role. This even extended to administering corporal punishment, not by borrowing the dominie's tawse, but perhaps in keeping with their army sergeant-major-like demeanour, with a short swagger cane. In many Scottish schools the janitor was very much the dominie's right-hand man and so in some, the right to discipline pupils was extended beyond the gymnasium, and there are mentions of janitors doling out punishment with their canes to latecomers.

Some dominies also regularly used their janitors as truant officers and it is perhaps not surprising to learn that they were often nicknamed 'whipper-ins'! In different parts of Scotland there were many different colloquial terms for playing truant. They included, 'wagging it', 'dogging it' and 'plugging it' and, more recently 'skiving' and 'bunking off'.

Mention earlier of physical education classes also recalls how adept the dominies' pupils were at finding different slang terms for gym shoes. Gym shoes should be known as plimsolls, taking their name from their inventor Samual Plimsoll, the Victorian Member of Parliament who introduced them to improve safety for sailors climbing the rigging on 19th-century ships like the *Cutty Sark*. In Glasgow schools they were often referred to as 'sannies', because the pupils often got them new, when they were about to go off 'doon the watter' for their annual Fair summer holidays in mid-July, as sand shoes to play on the beach or at least the shore at the various Clydeside resorts such as Dunoon, Largs, Rothesay and Millport and Brodick in Arran. In other schools in the West of Scotland they were usually called 'gutties', a rather ugly-sounding name probably derived from the fact that the soles of the gym shoes were made from a substance known as gutta-percha. Further east the soles of the pupils' gym shoes led them to nickname them 'rubbers', a name which led Dee Hepburn, the star of director Bill Forsythe's popular Scottish school film *Gregory's Girl*, having to spend a whole day in a New York dubbing studio substituting 'sneakers' as a more acceptable term, before the movie could be released for American audiences. *Gregory's Girl*, which was filmed at one of the new town of Cumbernauld's secondary schools, was also memorable for Scottish comedian, the late Chic Murray's portrayal of the absent-minded headmaster.

Another noteworthy portrayal of a Scottish dominie on the big screen came from another well-known comedian, Ricky Fulton, with his depiction of the school master in *Dollar Bottom*, which takes its title from his pupils' ingenious scheme to insure themselves against the infliction of corporal punishment. *Dollar Bottom* was based on a short story by the well-known Scottish dramatist, James Bridie.

Then there was also the dominie in the disappointing Hollywood film version of the musical *Brigadoon*, and the brief appearance of the dominie in the film version of Sir Compton MacKenzie's *Whisky Galore*. Pride of place in any list of silver screen dominies must, however, surely go to Alastair Sim's drag appearance as the headmistress in the *St Trinian's* series, inspired, it is claimed, by Ronald Searle's visit to a Scottish girls' boarding establishment of similar name which formerly occupied St Leonard's, the Victorian villa, at the entrance to Edinburgh University's Pollock Student Halls of Residence on the edge of the city's Holyrood Park.

On the small screen, the nearest Scottish dominies have reached to starring in a north of the border version of BBC Television's ever popular *Grange Hill* was Scottish Television's series, *This Man Craig*, which was set in a suburban Glasgow comprehensive secondary school. Set at the time when 'Guidance' was first introduced into Scottish schools in the 1960s, it sadly used this excuse to treat its teacher hero, played by the Scottish actor, John Cairney, as more of a roving social worker than a true chalkface dominie.

– 7 –
TAWSE TALES

'I was astonished at the amount of real pain inflicted and the length of time it lasted.'

Thus does David Daiches of the well-known Edinburgh Jewish legal family write in his autobiography, *Two Worlds*, about what he describes as his 'first experience with that instrument of torture, the tawse', as very effectively administered to him while he was a pupil in the primary department of the city's famous George Watson's College by his teacher, who he nicknamed Smiggles of H.

As he pulled back his maroon blazered arm and his almost equally purpled fingers, he continues:

> For over half an hour, my hand felt as though it were about a foot thick and the tips of my fingers, which felt like balloons, pulsed with agony. Then suddenly the pain changed into a warm glow and everything was very pleasant. I never bore any grudge against 'Smiggles of H'. She was, of course, only doing her duty.

Another Scottish dominie, who apparently definitely did 'his duty' with a vengeance was the Rector of the old High School of Edinburgh when Henry, Lord Cockburn, after whom the Cockburn Society is named, was a pupil at the close of the 18th century. For in his autobiography the famous Law Lord declares that, 'Out of the whole four years of my attendance, there were probably not ten days in which I was not flogged at least once.'

For centuries corporal punishment was a daily feature of Scottish school life and the dominies' rod of office was traditionally the long, lithe leather tawse.

The old adage that to spare the rod is to spoil the child definitely held sway and dominies were in fact often exhorted to wield the tawse more rather than less. The records of the Presbytery of St Andrews for the year 1661, for instance, state that the dominie at Beath was considered 'too lax in his exercise of discipline', and was 'too gentle in correcting the children' whose 'want of proficiency in learning' was deemed to stem from 'his want of firmness'.

Then in Dundee in 1674 the council decreed that if 'any scholar swear, break the Sabbath, or rebel against his master, he shall be publicly whipped for the first fault and flogged for any second'. What the difference was between a public whipping and a flogging is not described, but both sound suitably severe.

In 1679 the Provost and magistrates of Dunbar ordained that 'if a scholar becomes fugitive, the master shall punish him as he sees fit'. Later that same year the Dunbar councillors cracked down again on the boys of the burgh when they ruled that if 'scholars throw stones or snowballs, they shall be punished according to their deserts, especially if thrown at one another, or in the streets, or at or about dwelling houses'. The Dunbar dominie was also instructed to use his tawse on any 'scholars who use irritating words' and to use his discretion in strapping 'those who call nicknames'. While maintaining that they considered that 'the master who uses the tawse least uses it best', they then went on to tell the dominie that he was on no account 'to spare the child for his much crying'. Even an untidy appearance could result in a Dunbar laddie being strapped, because the town's councillors even laid down that those of them who were 'not neat in their clothes, and have not their hands and face washen, and their heads combed shall be slightly punished'.

The tawse took their unusual name from the method used to produce the supple leather required to manufacture these searing, stinging straps, used to chastise countless generations of Scottish bairns. It was described as 'tawing the hide', and the tawse was sometimes spelt taws or corrupted into tag or tards. No matter how it was described, however, the resounding smack of the tawse was undoubtedly the classroom clap of thunder, whose lightening swift strike cleared the air after any bout of misbehaviour. Much more controversially, the tawse were often used by many dominies to correct mistakes in pupils' work, from mis-spellings to wrong answers in the daily round of mental arithmetic.

The tawse were almost always referred to in the plural, sometimes as a pair of tawse, probably because the smacking punishment end of these two to three feet long implements for administering corporal punishment was always slashed into several slit thongs, designed to ensure each stroke inflicted the maximum tingling discomfort to the young recipient, without actually causing any lasting physical harm.

Effective beatings with the tawse were often described as 'good leatherings' and despite the undisputed pain were preferred by many Scottish pupils to the slow, non-physical punishments which replaced them after several European Court of Human Rights' rulings finally persuaded the government to ban all corporal punishment from Scottish local authority schools from August 1987. Many Scots of the older generation will, however, never forget the dominie's 'bit o' leather', which dominated their school days.

The list of offences for which dominies in other Scottish towns felt well justified in meting out punishment were equally many and varied. From the earliest times dominies were exhorted to whip pupils who played truant, came late to classes, threw stones or snowballs, carried weapons, told lies, swore or talked profanely, bullied or teased their fellows by calling them nicknames, played cards or dice or indulged in any other form of gambling.

The dominies were held to act *in loco parentis* and therefore had the same right as parents to use what was described as reasonable corporal chastisement. This right extended even beyond the classroom and the school day, and they were expected to discipline scholars for offences which occurred on the way to and from school and outside of school hours, such as failing to attend the kirk on the Sabbath.

The dominies' powers of discipline were really so extensive that Grant, in *The Burgh Schools Of Scotland*, ends by stating:

> The catalogue of transgressions which subjected the offender to punishment frequently concluded with a tail so comprehensive that masters seemed to have been invested with absolute powers; thus a catalogue of offences drawn up for the grammar school in Elgin in 1649, concludes with the penalties for those who shall be guilty of delinquencies within and insolences without the school.

It is therefore perhaps hardly surprising that one of the earliest written mentions of the tawse, which was recorded as long ago as 1639, was a complaint about their over harsh use by a Fife dominie. After considering the evidence, the Provost and the magistrates of the county town of Cupar warned 'the maister of the grammar school that he shall be removed from office if there be any repetition of the cruel exercise of discipline of the bairns in girding them to the blood'. The dominie appeared before the next meeting of the council and insisted that he was innocent, pleading that the fault was not his 'but that o' my new tawis. I never use it thaim befoir and found that they were our small maid.'

To claim that the weals inflicted on the boys and girls of Cupar were caused by too small, rather than too large a tawse, must seem a strange excuse to those who have never been at the receiving end of the dominie's bit o' leather, but his explanation was accepted by the magistrates of Cupar. For they recalled their own school days and like many a Scottish schoolchild since, realised full well that it is not the big broad belt that is to be feared, but the slender snake-like strap whose slit tongue really bites.

Why the Scottish dominies chose to chastise their erring scholars with the leather tawse rather than the curve-handled bamboo cane, or even the birch rod of their English counterparts, is lost in the chalk dust of antiquity. Perhaps it was simply that, thanks to the flourishing leather industry of medieval Scotland, it was easier to get hold of a handy piece of harness leather than a cane. A more academic origin was suggested however by James Grant M.A., the author of *History of the Burgh Schools of Scotland*, writing in 1876. For Grant, who was himself a teacher, was convinced that Scotland owed its instrument of school discipline, just like its famous legal system, to the Romans. He wrote:

> In our schools we have borrowed not only the literature, but with modifications, the instruments of discipline used by the Romans, who are believed to have carried the art of punishing to a high degree of perfection. Juvenal, in his Satires, speaks of one growing red under the scutica and their scutica was a scourge or whip made of leathern thongs. Even fiercer was the flagellum, called by Horace, 'horrible flagellum', which was a whip or lash of leathern thongs or twisted cords tied to a handle.

This reference to a wooden handle is particularly interesting because, while it is unlike any tawse used in schools in recent times, there are several mentions of just such instruments in the early records of several Scottish schools, including the High School of

Stirling, while even one hundred years ago the rector's tawse at the Royal High, Edinburgh was described as:

> more terrible than any of his masters as it consisted of leather lashes attached to a wooden handle, just like a miniature 'cat o' nine tails'.

Mention of this miniature cat o' nine tails has led other Scottish educational historians to suggest that Scottish school boys and girls should blame the tawse not on the Romans, but on the Auld Alliance between Scotland and France. For while corporal punishment is officially forbidden in all French schools, according to the women's magazine *Elle*, French parents make up for this absence of chastisement in the classroom by administering it themselves at home using a small wooden-handled multi-thonged whip called a 'martinet' after a very strict disciplinarian general in the French army. In French/English dictionaries 'martinet' is always described as a tawse.

While other European counties such as Sweden, Norway, Finland, Denmark and Austria have banned parents from so much as spanking their children, French mothers and fathers still believe in a *bonne fesse* and buy 300,000 martinets each year.

More a 'puss o' nine tails' than a cat, such instruments of chastisement, which French parents nowadays often prefer to claim they are buying to beat their furniture rather than their infants, are clearly therefore as much a French tradition as the tawse is in Scotland and the suggestion is that way back in history one was brought to the royal court at Holyrood by one of the many courtiers who came to stay there during the regency of Mary of Guise. This unusual outcome of the Auld Alliance gains support from the fact that a payment for 'taws' does appear in the records of Linlithgow Palace, which was given to the French queen as part of her dowry, and where she often used to stay.

Whether the first tawse came from France or from the Romans, there is no doubt that the word chosen by Scottish bairns to describe its strokes has a classical origin.

'Pande manum' commanded the dominie, using Latin, which was the accepted language of the old grammar school classroom, to order 'Hold out your hand'; and so from 'Pande manum' came 'Pandies', the word used by Scottish pupils to describe the strokes of the tawse.

But in some schools, knowledge of Latin was not as good as in others and so 'Pandies' became 'Pawmies', or even 'Palmies', after the part of the pupil's anatomy most often chosen as the target area. In some parts of Scotland, especially in the south-west, as in Walter Wingate's poem, pupils also used to call smacks of the strap 'liffies', which was their corruption of 'loofs' or 'luifs', meaning the palms of their hands. But although the tawse was latterly almost always inflicted across the palm and fingers of pupils' hands, in previous centuries it was just as often administered on the bottom and perhaps, even more painfully, across the backs of pupils' legs.

In 1640 for instance, in Dundonald in Ayrshire, the dominie was instructed by the bailies and magistrates 'to punish according to the quality of the faults, striking some on the hand with a birch wand or pair of taws, others on the hips, as their faults deserve'.

Writing in *The Burgh Schools of Scotland*, James Grant again stated that he personally knew 'an old fashioned dominie, who punished his scholars by fastening them upon a bench at the door and removing their clothes before skelping them with his tawse'.

Mr Grant also described how, at Dundee High School where the tawse was administered across the legs, 'the boys not long ago protected the calves of their legs by using their book boards, which they placed within the legs of their trousers'.

Like the Dundee laddies, many pupils obviously believed that prevention was better than cure, for Mr Grant also tells the tale of one Scot who went through life with the nickname 'Leather Doup' because when he was wee he persuaded his mother to sew a sheep's skin inside the seat of his trousers to diminish the sting of the dominie's leatherings.

In some Aberdeenshire schools there was a large flat stone just outside the door to which pupils who had been chastised could rush at playtimes to sit and take some of the heat out of their wounds, this earning for it the nickname of 'the cooling stane'.

One school adjoined the graveyard and the kirk session protested to the dominie that his scholars were using one of the grave stones 'for this unbefitting purpose'.

They didn't go on to demand that the dominie get to the bottom of it, and, in fact, why the Scottish maisters changed their *modus operandi* from the seat to the hand is not recorded. It seems probable, however, that it may have been the increase in the number of girls attending the parish schools which saved the boys from such indignities and persuaded the dominies to confine the use of the tawse to the palms, upon which part of their anatomy the lassies could, and did, receive their fair share of chastisement when their behaviour, or rather their misbehaviour, warranted it.

The change from bottoms to hands may not have pleased the boys so much, however, for it must have made it much more difficult for them to escape from the full force of the tawse. Try they did, however, with suggestions ranging from laying a horse hair across their fingers, to rubbing their palms with bacon fat or even a slice of raw onion, which was alleged to cut down the pain. More practical perhaps was the well-known habit of spitting on the hands, but whether this was best done before or after getting the punishment was always a matter of dispute. Other boys and girls placed their faith in heating their palms beforehand by rubbing them feverishly up and down the pipes of the old-fashioned classroom heating pipes or more modern night store heaters, while standing directly below the blackboard light so that the teacher could not take a full swing was also a favourite trick of the classroom 'artful dodgers'.

Dodging was, of course, the most popular form of avoiding action of all. This consisted of pulling away the palm, so that it appeared to have been well and truly strapped, but was in truth practically unscathed. This was a skill of which not a few pupils were very proud, some even contriving to add the right sound effects by cupping their hands so that the trapped air exploded and made it sound as if the culprit had been well and truly executed.

On the other hand, so to speak, other pupils seemed to take an almost perverse pleasure in taking the full force of the tawse. Take, for instance, young Kenn in Neil Gunn's *Highland River*.

The Master was a man who must have measured six feet three inches and weighed seventeen stone. He was straight and agile and unthinkably strong; brown-haired with a full, smooth, blood-flushed face, and pale-blue eyes that occasionally had threads in them, though he never drank or smoked. He was probably under fifty years of age.

Now as he watched the smile dawn on Kenn's face, the fleshly stentorian abruptness of his expression held, then wavered, and finally passed into a small answering smile, not of reverie or gentleness, but of acute humour. A pucker came upon his face; his eyes glinted. He stopped right before Kenn and in a private voice asked, 'What's the smile for?'

Kenn gave a compulsive start, his eyes shooting to the master's face; then confused, he drooped over his book.

'Eh?, What was it?' The voice was quiet and friendly.

But like some adventuring whelk touched on the raw, Kenn wanted to withdraw out of sight. The only thing he could hide behind, however, was his face, so it produced its dour and hostile shell.

'What was it?' The voice was firmer, but still searching for human contact.

'Nothing', muttered Kenn.

There was a moment of silence in which the whole room could be heard listening.

'Nothing WHAT?' suggested the master.

'Nothing, Sir',

'So you were smiling at nothing?'

Kenn did not answer.

The master's expression hardened. The glint in his eyes became concentrated and hostile. 'So you were smiling at nothing?' His voice had risen. There was a pause, then an explosive roar in which the moment of possible communion was shattered to fragments.

'I'll make you smile at something!' 'Come out here.'

Kenn went out.

Swiftly with thunderous steps, the master had plunged to his desk and returned with the three fingered leather strap. 'Hold it out!'

Kenn held his arm the full length and took the regulation three on his palm. They stung with blinding fierceness for the master put all his strength into the strokes. Kenn's eyelids quivered but he made no sound.

The second time Kenn got thrashed was for transposing the products of Birmingham and Leicester. 'I'll give you Leicester!' said the master. This time Kenn whimpered, for his palm was swollen and tender, and, moreover he knew that the master was now being vindictive.

The whimper had an angry rebellious edge to it, which the master recognised as protest. This infuriated him.

So he made Kenn hold out his other hand, and though he should now have given him only two, he actually put extra pith into a third.

At least poor Kenn only received his punishment single handed. Many teachers believed that they could make each punishment even sorer by insisting on pupils holding out both hands at the same time. For 'cross handers' or 'doublers' as boys and girls called this form of punishment, one hand had to be laid directly on top of the other, palms up. Some teachers made pupils interlace their fingers so that both hands were actually strapped by the same stroke, but most were content simply to rely on the hand underneath to prevent the boy or girl pulling away the one on top.

Most children considered 'doublers' fair, but another method by which some teachers greatly increased the pain of the tawse was considered definitely 'below the belt', as they might have put it. This consisted of making the child place his hand, palm uppermost, not out in front of him but flat upon the desk. This, pupils always felt, took any sporting chance out of a strapping, for there was absolutely no chance of pulling the palm out of the way.

Happily most teachers disdained any such subterfuge, considering administering the tawse really quite an art, which consisted of ensuring just the required degree of stinging discomfort without leaving the slightest mark. Reddening the palms was alright, but leaving weals, especially on the wrists, was not. One of the merits of the tawse, as an instrument of child chastisement, was always considered to be its ability to carry out its unpleasant duty without leaving any lasting injury, unlike the English cane, whose strokes could more accurately be described as cuts.

Brute force never entered into effective strapping. The secret lay in a subtle flick of the wrist at just the right moment and a good eye for distance, which accounted for the fact that even the slightest of lady teachers could command respect from the toughest of teenage classes, especially if she just happened to be known to have a low handicap at the local golf course.

And every bit as much care often went into choosing a tawse as went into picking a new set of irons. At first every local saddler no doubt produced a tawse when called upon to do so by the local dominie, but gradually the prowess of certain saddlers for producing specially supple and stingy straps became well known and teachers were prepared to travel miles to obtain the right weapon.

In his *Daft Days*, Neil Munro had his two school ma'ams, the Misses Duff, travel to Edinburgh to buy their very first tawse and portrayed their confused blushing embarrassment as their newly-purchased instrument of chastisement fell from the coach 'and uncoiled, hideous and serpent-like on the public highway in full view of the visiting American'.

But in real life it was to the little Fife mining village of Lochgelly that most punishment pilgrimages were made.

For it was in his tiny workshop, behind his ironmonger's, stocked with all the usual everyday household items, that John Dick became the high priest of punishment. Any thought of finding a sinister Scottish Marquis de Sade are, however, quickly dispelled, for Mr Dick was a mild-mannered, quietly-spoken white-haired gentleman. He inherited his tawse-making business from his father, who, in turn, had taken it over after working for the original Lochgelly saddler, Mr George Philips, who began the whole tawse connection when his daughter, who was a local schoolteacher, asked him to make her a good strap. Orders soon followed from other members of her school staff and then from teachers in many other schools in Fife. Before long, orders began to come in from schools all over Scotland and even from Scottish dominies exiled in other parts of the world, until the name of the wee coal mining village of Lochgelly became synonymous for the best made tawse that money could buy.

What made the 'Lochgelly Specials', as they were always called, even after John Dick moved the family business to the larger neighbouring town of Cowdenbeath, so effective, was apparently a combination of factors. For their straps the Philips, and later the Dicks, always selected the very top quality of supple flexible leather known as buffalo butts, although it was actually horse hide. Then experience of producing so very many tawse taught them exactly the right way to slash the smacking end into the much feared thongs. Finally, and most importantly, every single tawse was carefully hand finished. Thus a teacher was guaranteed that he could wield a 'Lochgelly Special' or 'Lochgelly Repeater', as they were sometimes also nicknamed, because of their sharp pistol-like crack, as they delivered each stroke, without the risk of any angry red marks on young recipients and resulting visits from even angrier parents.

There were however, 'Lochgelly Specials' and 'Lochgelly Specials', because Mr Dick actually produced a whole range of school straps, so that he could always supply a suitable punishment tool for both teacher and taught. The available 'Lochgellies' therefore started with a twenty-one inch long, light-weight, two-thonged model for use in the days when corporal punishment was meted out even in infant classrooms. For older primary boys and girls, teachers then had a choice of keeping to a light-weight strap but with three thongs, or switching to thicker and heavier medium-weight two and three thonged models.

Secondary teachers could obtain longer two-foot medium-weight straps, the extra inches delivering extra velocity to the strokes, but the real sting came when they switched to the heavy and extra heavy-weight 'Lochgellies', designed to strike terror into the hearts and hands of even the most troublesome fifteen-year-old school leavers. The extra heavy 'Lochgelly' had thongs thick enough for it to stand upright on the teacher's desk as a very visible ultimate deterrent.

The thongs were the thing which always added to the terror of the tawse. The secret of its searing sting lay in these slit tongues, which the dominies of old were convinced enabled it to communicate so much more effectively than angry words to the young delinquents who it chastised. The fact that the punishment end was slashed cut down air resistance, just as is the case with the pattern of holes drilled into the spanking part of the punishment paddles favoured by teachers in American schools, but exactly how many thongs made a tawse most effective was long the subject of staffroom debate and playground dispute. Examples of tawse, preserved for all to see in the Victorian classroom at Gladstone Court Museum in Biggar, and in local museums in many other Scottish towns, have as many as five, six or even seven long slender thongs, and rather like the funnels on ocean liners of bygone days extra thongs appeared to give added status to teachers' straps, especially as far as pupils were concerned.

During the final years of the use of corporal punishment in Scottish schools, however, both John Dick in Lochgelly, and the other main producer of tawse, Brownlee, the Saddler of Bathgate, who regularly advertised their school straps in the teachers' weekly newspaper, the *Educational Institute of Scotland Journal*, always insisted on a maximum of three.

Just as the number of thongs on the tawse decreased in recent years, so too did the number of strokes which it was customary to inflict. In Scottish schools of the fifties, sixties and seventies, six well applied cross-handers was considered a very severe and serious punishment, but this cannot compare with some of the strappings recorded in the past.

One of the most brutal was that recorded by the Scottish poet Alexander Smart, who died in 1866. Describing his school days in Montrose, he tells of the day he incurred the full wrath of his dominie, the grim and terrible Mr Norval:

> Every Saturday Mr Norval caused his pupils to repeat a prayer which he had composed for their use, and on hearing which he stood over each with a paper ruler ready in the unfortunate event of omission of word or phrase, to strike down the unfortunate offender, who all the while stooped tremblingly before him. On one of these days of extorted prayer, I was found at fault with my grammar lesson, and the offence was deemed worthy of peculiar castigation.
>
> The school was dismissed at the usual time, but along with a few other boys, who were to become witnesses of my punishment and disgrace, I was detained in the classroom, and dragged to the presence of the tyrant. Despite every effort, I resisted being bound to a bench and flogged after the fashion of the time. So the punishment was commuted into 'palmies'. Horrible commutation! Sixty lashes with leather thongs on my right hand, inflicted with all the severity of my tyrant's wrath, made me scream in the agony of desperation. My pitiless tormentor, unmoved by the sight of my hand sorely lacerated and swollen to twice its natural size, threatened to cut out my tongue, if I continued to complain and so saying laid hold of a pair of scissors and inflicted a deep wound on my lip.

The fact that young Smart was ordered to stay behind after class to receive his beating was unusual because mostly dominies punished as soon as offences came to their notice and the immediacy of corporal punishment was always held to be one of its advantages over slower non-physical sanctions, which rely on depriving pupils of their free time for their effect. Charles Thomson, President of the Educational Institute of Scotland during the 1930s notes in his autobiographical book, *Scottish School Humour*, that at his suburban Glasgow city school, minor offences were punished straight away but that:

> the headmaster usually allowed the severer punishments to accumulate till a certain hour in the afternoon. Then the culprits had to proceed in Indian file round and round a certain clump of desks for a number of times corresponding to the number of whacks each was to receive. If he missed you, it was his fault, and you counted as having gone round once all the same. Great was the ingenuity displayed in sprinting up to within a foot of the thrashing point, suddenly pausing till the stroke fell, and then rushing on again for the next round. Once we had the fearful joy of seeing a regular chase by the headmaster after one of the big boys, round the desks, out through and round the playground and back round the desks again, until final capture brought the inevitable punishment. Besides the tawse there was used on occasion that abominable weapon, the cane.

Mention of the cane being used in a Glasgow local authority school is unusual as the city's education authority had the strictest rules in Scotland on corporal punishment. It was the only education authority to lay down that its teachers use special regulation tawse manufactured in the city by saddlers J. and G. Stevenson. Although Stevenson's black tawse were longer than the famous 'Lochgellies', they were made of lighter-weight leather and Glasgow teachers, especially in the tougher secondary schools, often risked smuggling in the 'specials' from Fife. Perhaps the dominie at Mr Thomson's primary school thought he had found a loophole in the Glasgow corporal punishment regulations, not by using a different make of tawse which the rules forbade, but by importing a cane, whose use they did not mention.

Caning is also mentioned occasionally in Scottish Roman Catholic schools, perhaps because some of their teachers came from the south of Ireland where that was the usual mode of chastisement. A former pupil of St Joseph's Primary School, Linlithgow, recalls that:

> By today's standards, I suppose our teachers, although devoted, were strict. They stood absolutely no nonsense. All three used the cane. The girls had to do something pretty serious to be called out to be caned, but the boys got it every day for everything from mistaken spelling to any classroom misbehaviour. When I was in the top class I was several times

given the job of going to buy new canes. They were always purchased from Hebsons the ironmongers in Linlithgow High Street. Picking the right canes was a difficult task. If I returned with canes which were too small, the teacher would send me straight back to the shop, but if they were too thick the other boys were none too pleased. Strangely enough they were happy when the teachers got new canes, because to begin with these new lengths of bamboo were never as painful as the old ones, which always hurt more as they frayed at the ends and split thus doubling the sting.

The use of the cane at the Linlithgow Catholic school ceased in 1927 when a new headmaster was appointed, and although from England, he introduced the tawse as already used in the West Lothian county town's other local schools.

Other peculiarly Roman Catholic variations from the Scottish normal method of administering corporal punishment were very much a feature of school life at St Aloysius College, Glasgow's famous Jesuit seat of learning. There the traditional instrument of discipline was a distinct variation of the tawse called the 'ferula', a Latin term which had sometimes been used in other Scottish schools in the Middle Ages. Like a normal tawse the ferula was made of leather, but the boys of St Aloysius always swore that the black leather only covered its real hidden deterrent — a length of flexible whale bone, similar, but shorter than the whale bones used in the manufacture of Irish teachers' dreaded pandybats.

Unlike the usual solid leather tawse, the ferula may well indeed have had a different core, because it is always described as being sewn with stitches round the edges, which added to the pain which it inflicted, and whether or not its hidden secret was truly whale bone, it was apparently a formidable instrument of punishment. One former Jesuit schoolboy described it as 'Narrow in the middle and thick at both ends so that it had none of the cutting effect of a cane. It was administered with very rare exceptions, on the palms of the hand. While it was painful at the time, the soreness soon passed off if you pressed your hands into a hot water pipe. There was never any danger of lasting damage.'

Apart from utilising such a different instrument to maintain discipline, St Aloysius, like other Jesuit schools, used a different system to ensure it was administered with strict impartiality. Boys were never chastised by the teacher whom they had offended or who had found fault with their work. When a boy was sentenced to so many strokes, the teacher wrote the punishment down on a piece of paper called a bill, and that was the last he had to do with the matter. The guilty boy was then on his honour to pay for his misdeed, or lack of work, by presenting his bill to the school's Prefect of Discipline within twenty-four hours of it being issued. There were set times of the school day at St Aloysius when the Prefect was available with his ferula at the ready to accept bills and administer the required number of whacks, and to add to the anticipated agony boys usually had to queue and await their turn in grim anticipation of how sore it was going to be.

When at last the boy entered the Prefect's study he handed over his bill. The Prefect read it and impersonally entered the stated number of strokes in the punishment book. Then producing the dreaded ferula from beneath the folds of his soutane, he took hold of the boy's hand and extended it to full length. Taking aim he then brought the broad rounded end of the ferula cracking down on the outstretched palm.

The final difference at St Aloysius was the number of stokes of the ferula to which boys were sentenced, which were usually greater than at other schools. A former pupil recalls that:

> The tariff began at three and advanced by three strokes at a time. While six of the ferula was normal, nine, twelve and sometimes even fifteen strokes was not unusual. The worst punishment of all was what on a bill was described as "twice nine". That meant eighteen painful strokes, always administered with the full force of the ferula, nine searing smacks on each hand, but that was reserved for the most serious offences. It was, of course, the talk of the school when such a bill was issued, but normally the distinct crack of the ferula was just accepted as a normal background noise to every morning playtime and lunchtime at the school. We knew the Prefect was simply doing his duty and never bore him any grudge, simply admiring his skill at ensuring the required amount of pain, without leaving any lasting tell tale marks, apart from the flaming redness of our fingers, which even if you waited to cash your bill at the lunchtime session, had all but disappeared by the end of afternoon school, so you

never had the satisfaction of showing your mother or in the older classes even your girl friend how you had suffered.

The ferula was abolished at St Aloysius during the 1980s at about the same time that girls were admitted as pupils for the first time, two changes which many old boys still regret.

Another Scottish school in the independent sector with both an unusual style of administering corporal punishment and an equally unusual implement to do so was Edinburgh Academy. In his autobiography, well-known writer and former pupil, the late Alan Melville, describes it as follows.

> There is an institution at Edinburgh Academy called the clachan. It is really an item of sporting equipment, consisting of a flat oval-shaped piece of hardwood on the end of a long stick, but it can be used for non-sportive purposes — mainly discipline, which at the Academy, unless the crime was a really serious one, was dealt out by the senior boys on the behinds of the juniors. Friday night was torture night.

Melville then goes on to tell of his own first personal encounter at the receiving end of the clachan as wielded by his head of house. He writes:

> He suddenly said, 'Right: bend over', and gave me six absolute belters with his clachan. 'The trouble with you,' he said, 'is that you're wet.' I went straight to the bogs and cried my eyes out. Not at the effect of the clachan, though my backside was still stinging, but at being called wet.

The infliction of corporal punishment in Scottish schools did however, on occasion, also have its more light-hearted moments. One such is the true tale of a dominie whose lesson was interrupted by persistent whistling coming from the playground immediately below his classroom. Angrily he ordered the culprit to come up to his room. 'Hold out your hands, double', he ordered, and despite the boy's muttered protests strapped him soundly, before the poor unfortunate lad was able to get through to him that he had in fact left school the previous Friday and had just finished his first shift in the local pit!

Fortunately the punishment was taken in good part by the young miner, as were the vast majority of Scottish school strappings. There was, in fact, a tradition that for a child to confess to having been strapped in school was to invite a further leathering at home.

'You must have deserved it' was the attitude of most Scottish parents, but sometimes complaints did occur. One of the most famous was that recorded by Sir Walter Scott in his journal on 13 December 1826 when he wrote:

> Went to court this morning and remained till past three. Then attended a meeting of Edinburgh Academy rectors on account of some discussion about flogging. I am an enemy of corporal punishment, but there are many boys, who will not attend without it. It is an instant and irresistible motive and I love boys' heads too much to spoil them at the expense of their opposite extremity. Then when children feel an emancipation on this point, we may justly fear they will loose the bonds of discipline altogether. I was indifferently well beaten at school, but now I am quite certain that twice as much discipline would have been well bestowed.

Another early attempt to ban the tawse took a very different form altogether from that desired by modern abolitionists with their appeals to the European Court of Human Rights, for far from sparing the child, this Victorian effort to ban the belt aimed to replace it with a real rod.

This proposal was put forward in a parliamentary bill introduced into the House of Lords in 1869 by the Marquis of Townshend, who called for the birch rod to be the only instrument of chastisement used in schools, as his lordship, no doubt from experience, thought that it was much safer than 'inflicting cuts of the cane.'

Fortunately for Scottish bairns faced with this painful alternative to the tawse, the Earl of Airlie was quickly on his feet to defend Scotland's time-honoured length of leather, and in the end the birch bill was withdrawn.

The publicity given to the House of Lords' discussion did, however, lead several English education authorities, including Newcastle, Manchester and Walsall, to allow their teachers to use the tawse as an alternative to the cane, of which Lord Townshend had been so critical.

The matter also attracted attention in the medical press, and then, and on several occasions up until 1937, when the whole question of corporal punishment, including court floggings and birchings, was very much in the headlines, the Scottish tawse was judged the safest instrument with which to chastise children. One of England's leading leather manufacturing towns, Walsall, continued to permit its teachers to punish with the tawse until the 1980s, a fact which led to its education authority being reported to the European Court of Human Rights by a local mother. She complained that her children, including her daughter, had been smacked several times with the tawse both on their hands and bottoms. Again, interestingly, in the defence evidence the local medical officer of health stressed the safety record of the tawse in comparison with any other means of administering corporal punishment.

The European Court awarded compensation to the mother on the grounds that the school had failed to take into account her philosophical views against physical punishment, but did not support her claims that the use of the tawse had been cruel or degrading, something it consistently declined to do in any of the Scottish or English school punishment cases taken before it.

Despite this, however, the British government, by a majority of one single vote at the close of a House of Commons debate on the subject in July 1986, felt sufficiently pressured to ban all forms of corporal punishment in local authority schools as of August the following year.

Ironically however, more than ten years later old fashioned tawse are still being manufactured, not only to supply the few schools in the private independent fee paying sector in this country where their use is still legal, but because there is a small but steady demand for these leather chastisers from other countries in the world, including several in Africa, the West Indies, some states in Australia, and lands in the Far East where the lessons of emigrant Scottish dominies and their methods from past years still hold sway and which still believe that a smack in time stops crime.

Perhaps the best ending to these tawse tales would be to suggest a compromise, which is summed up by another proverb, this time an old Scottish one, which says, 'Ne'er wield the tawse, when a gloom will dae the trick.'

CHAPTER 8
THE INSPECTOR COMES TO CALL

Nothing strikes a visitor to the Scotch schools so much as the want of organisation and defective discipline, which prevails to a very great extent. We found a large number of schools, where it was impossible to carry out the work of examination until half of the children were dismissed and in school they were constantly disorderly and careless in their appearance and manner. They lolled about the benches, sat and stood with their caps on their heads and their hands in their pockets, talking to each other and playing tricks upon their neighbours. In the playground they were very rough and unmannerly and not unfrequently indecent and all these minor immoralities were unchecked by the teachers, who seemed to consider they had nothing to do with the civilisation of the children or the formation of their characters, but that the work was done, when they heard them say their daily lessons in the schoolroom.

Thus reported the 1865 Education Commission following the inspection of 133 parish schools in 17 Scottish counties.

The first Government Inspectors Report on schools was published in 1842, but long before the appointment of professional HMIs, Scottish dominies had to put up with frequent visitations from a considerable array of local dignitaries, all of whom considered that they knew exactly how the bairns ought to be taught their lessons, even if they themselves in many cases appeared to have failed to learn many during their own school days.

Amongst those who carried out these early visitations were the local laird, the parish minister, the Kirk Session, the Provost, the Magistrates and the Councillors. It is a pity that they were seldom the 'discreet, learned and grave men' whom John Knox called for in his *Book of Discipline* to carry out quarterly visitations. What they may have lacked in expertise and brain power, these early inspectors made up for in pomp, solemnity and ceremony, with their appearances being significant events in the life of every school, dreaded by both masters and pupils alike.

It seems inconceivable that any other professional group such as lawyers or doctors would have put up with the amount of interference forced upon the dominies, and to this day Scottish education is still suffering from a hangover of amateur do-gooders such as the famous county councillor who, when interviewing an applicant for a top rectorship asked, 'I see you're an Honours graduate, but hae ye passed your Highers?'

How negative some of the early inspections were is illustrated by the rules drawn up by Edinburgh magistrates for visitations of the High School in 1640. First they decreed that 'there be set down ane solid course for the tryell of the maister and doctors in teaching and attending of the scholleris concreddit to their care', and that having heard each pupil 'turn a theame', the boys were to be dismissed so that the examiners could 'remove the maister to see if anything can be found against him'. Later, the assistant masters, or doctors, as they were always described, were also to be interrogated to discover any faults, which were to be rectified by the full council.

In most places school visitations took place twice a year, at the beginning of May, and at the end of October. But in some places, such as Paisley and Aberdeen, they were inflicted upon the master and his scholars as often as once a month. In 1791, at Fortrose Academy, visitations were made weekly, and in case this was not sufficient to keep the dominie and his pupils constantly on their toes it was decreed that there should be twice yearly public examination of all scholars by all members of the Presbytery.

During these regular inspections the master had to submit a list of all the Latin texts which he claimed to have taught, and any of the visitors was then free to examine the pupils on any part of them. Frequently this was a great temptation for the visitors to try to show off their own learning by asking the most obtuse questions.

In addition to the regular visitations to test the master's teaching and the boys' learning, special inspections were often made to ensure that discipline was being strictly maintained. The first recorded inspection of Perth Grammar School in 1630 was held to find ways of improving the discipline of the pupils, while in Stirling, when the councillors felt that behaviour was not all that it might be in the burgh schools they invited the local ministers to 'concur and go along' to back them up in urging the masters to be more dutiful in enforcing the rules.

Other towns in which the councillors felt that discipline was so 'decayed' in their schools as to call for special inspections include Montrose, Cupar and Dundee , where in 1749 the magistrates seem almost disappointed to have to record that they had found the English school 'better than they had expected', but resolve 'to try again the proficiency of the boys at Lammas next', in case it was only a temporary improvement.

During the second half of the 18th century the growth of newspapers enabled the results of school inspections to be published. Usually these accounts were pretty complimentary to the dominie, but the magistrates were not adverse to administering a public rebuke if they considered it necessary, as was the case in Ayr in 1784 when they noted that 'the few scholars in the mathematical class have made little progress, owing to the want of authority of the master'.

By the beginning of the 19th century a practice which must have kept both masters and boys absolutely on tenterhooks right up to the moment school broke up for the summer holidays appears to have become common throughout Scotland. This was the public examination of the pupils on the morning of the last day of term. Inevitably the masters tried to make their scholars seem as bright as possible, and often answers as well as questions were carefully rehearsed in the hope that the official visitors, having been suitably wined and entertained beforehand, would be content to allow the dominie to conduct the whole show. And a show many of these end-of-term inspections undoubtedly became with pupils being carefully taught the parts of the piece which they would be called upon to recite. Gradually these end-of-term visitations changed from inspections to end-of-term concerts, with prizes for those who performed best, and one school which until recently kept up this old custom by holding its prize giving on the final morning of term was Linlithgow Academy.

In any case, by this time the need for formal visitations by councillors and ministers was at an end, for from 1840 onwards six officially appointed Government inspectors covered the whole of

Scotland. If anything, however, visits from these grim black-clad gentlemen were feared even more than the previous amateur visitations, for they now had the power to withhold the new government grant from any school which did not meet with their satisfaction.

As professional inspectors they should have been better qualified than the local magistrates to examine and pass judgement on the schools, but from the outset they were viewed with suspicion by the dominies who complained that instead of experienced school masters, the Government favoured ex-army types with the right accent, but no knowledge of either children or teaching for the new jobs, and to some extent similar criticism has haunted the HMIs to the present day.

Perhaps it was because of their scorn for the professional experience of the HMIs that so many of the dominies appear to have to have been quite willing to trick the inspectors whenever possible. The commonest way in which the dominies tried to make a good impression when the inspector asked them to take a class lesson was to tell the children to put up their hands for every question, whether or not they really knew the answer. This not only looked impressive to the inspector, but sounded as if the class really knew their lessons, for the dominie made sure that every answer was a correct one by carefully instructing the boys and girls beforehand that they were to put up their right hands if they knew the answer, but their left hands if they were just pretending.

Another trick was to make sure that every child had one correct answer well battered into his head the day before, and then to ask them each in the correct order when the inspector was present the following day. This could, of course, be a risky business, as one dominie found to his cost when, while being inspected during a history lesson, he asked, 'And at what battle did the Duke of Wellington defeat Napoleon?' Quick as a flash a hand shot up, but little did the dominie realise that this was to be his Waterloo. For instead of the name of the battle, the answer which he received was 'Please Sir, the laddie who knows that is no here the day.'

Sometimes the Inspector himself asked the questions, but this too was fraught with difficulties such as the occasion in a Border country school when an HMI showed a class of infants a drawing of a sheep. 'Now I'm sure you can all tell what kind of animal this is' he declared, only to be met with dead silence. 'Come along now, I'm sure many of your fathers keep these on their farms' he continued helpfully. At last one hand went up hesitantly. 'Weil its maybe a Cheviot or a Border Leicester' replied the wee laddie, 'but if ma faither had a beast like yon on oor fairm, he'd be aw for sending the herd to the slaughter hoose instead o' the sheep.'

Another inspector who met his match in a country school was the one who showed the class a picture of a frog. 'What animal have we here' he asked?

'A puddock' they all replied.

'No, no, not puddock' he coaxed.

Mystified the boys and girls looked round until one plucked up courage and shoved up his hand.

'I'll bet you a bob it's a puddock' he declared.

If the pupils were ever lost for words the inspectors were not, for after each visit the dominie could be certain to receive a long written report which had to be read to the school board and carefully copied into the log book.

Here is one typical report:

In the Junior Division spelling requires increased attention, which in the lower classes is of too ambitious a character, and is of not more than average merit. Oral arithmetic is good but in some of the higher classes written arithmetic admits of improvement. In class 2 arithmetic and spelling require closer attention. Composition is of a creditable quality, but is somewhat unequal. In the three highest classes a deliberate and expressive style of reading and recitation has become general and paper work is neat and careful. It may he pointed out, however, that the boys' speech might be less rough and indistinct, that the arithmetic of class 2 should improve in speed and accuracy and that classes 1a and 1b might have a firmer grasp of fractions.

In the supplementary classes the boys' writing is somewhat cramped and irregular, but the written exercises of the girls were very neat and careful. Composition in both classes merits a word of praise. The boys showed a creditable proficiency in the elements of geometry and the girls gave a very good exhibition of physical drill.

– 9 –
THE DOMINIE AT HOME

'The school master has the legal accommodation.' This bald statement occurs repeatedly in the descriptions of parishes in the *Second Statistical Account of Scotland* published during the 1840s, but what were the dominies' school houses really like?

The custom of providing a school house in each parish for the dominie dates back to the secularisation of Scottish education at the time of the Reformation in the middle of the 16th century. The provision of a school house helped compensate for the low salaries which the dominies were paid.

Often these early school houses were supplied furnished and a detailed inventory for one of them still exists. It describes the very basic 'plenishment' of the school house in Peebles in 1688. The list of furnishings details:

One bed, with a bottom; one vessel ambrie (cupboard) at the bedside; one table; one pantry, beneath the stair, with lock and key; one little ambrie above the pantry door; one shelf within the chamber; one door on the chamber with sneck and lock; one door on the loft with lock and key; a partition wall coming into the hall; a lock, sneck and shot on the outer door; sufficient glass windows in the hall and chamber.

Presumably the dominie had to supply his own chair or stool to sit at the table, because none is mentioned, and presumably if married the dominie and his wife supplied additional pieces of their own furniture to make the school house more of a home.

There is evidence that some dominies maintained well-furnished school houses from the fact that when the provost and magistrates of Linlithgow dismissed one of Scotland's most famous grammar school masters, Alexander Kirkwood, author of the well-known Latin text book, for refusing to worship in the Protestant manner, he protested very vocally about them throwing his fine carved wooden dining room table and chairs and other items, which had come from the Continent, out of the school house and into the street. Rector Kirkwood may have had a particularly well-furnished school house because of his marriage to his Dutch wife, Golentine van Beest, who may have brought some of the items from her family home in the Netherlands.

Parishes which did not supply a school house for their dominie appear to have adopted various different alternatives instead. Most common was to pay the dominie what was described as 'chalmer maill', so that he could afford to rent a suitable room or chamber in the neighbourhood of his school.

In some of the parishes, which lacked school houses, however, in order to avoid even the expense of paying 'chalmer maill', the members of the kirk session or the local councillors decided that parents must take it in turn to provide the dominie with bed and board in their own homes. Two places in Fife, where this was the custom, were Burntisland and Crail. In 1571 it is recorded that the dominie in Crail had his 'meat and daily sustentation' from different families in turn, while in Burntisland in 1596 the parents of pupils were required 'to lodge the master in their homes by turns'.

In Stirling parents were given the choice of paying an extra six shillings quarterly or of accommodating and feeding the master for two days each quarter if they had one child at school, or for four days if two children attended classes. If they had three children at school, however, they were still only required to provide the dominie with four days' meat and board, but four or more children in attendance guaranteed the master food and a roof over his head for six days each quarter.

How the school master felt about having to make such frequent 'flittings', to use the good old Scottish word for moving house, is not recorded, but the reluctance of many of the mothers and fathers to provide hospitality is apparent from the burgh records of several towns. In Haddington in 1590, for instance, parents with children attending the town's grammar school, who refused to provide bread and board for the assistant master were fined eight pence each. In Stirling in 1602 the town council ordered one of the bailies to inform all of the families with children attending the town's grammar school that 'if the master be neglected' they would be liable to be fined six shillings and eight pence and that this fine would be used to compensate the teacher.

One of the last towns in Scotland to continue this custom of boarding the dominie was Sanquhar in Dumfriesshire, where as late as 1691, parents were expected to provide the dominie with a full week's accommodation, the number of times a year that the master came to stay with each family depending on how many of their sons and daughters were attending the school.

While no reference to families in towns having to entertain the dominie has come to light after 1700, the practice did continue throughout the 18th century in rural areas, and according to Grant, in his book on parish and village schools, it still continued into the 19th century. Writing in 1876 he stated:

> The practice of boarding the teacher, long extinct in the towns, prevailed till recently, at least in some of our rural districts. A group of families, living in some sequestered spot, too distant from the parish school, having secured the services of a lad possessed of the requisite modicum of schooling, a school room was fitted up in some central place, while the teacher himself was boarded and lodged at each house in the hamlet or clachan in regular rotation for a week, fortnight or month at a time as might be arranged. We remember two of the itinerant or occasional teachers who shared our family meal in the Davoch of Inchbraon and they assured us that they enjoyed their wanderings immensely, not withstanding the frequency of the flittings. This arrangement could not fail to be of mutual benefit to the teacher, parents and scholars — the former, by his constant change of residence and the part he took in their employments and amusements becoming acquainted with the varied characters and dispositions of his constituents, while the latter naturally had their interest in the work of the school intensified by frequent intercourse with the master.

Even where dominies officially had school houses of their own, there must have been occasions when they felt they saw much too much of their scholars, because there were examples during the 17th and 18th centuries of buildings where there were no proper partitions between the domestic apartments, where they ate and slept, and the classrooms, where they taught their pupils during the day. In Monkton, Ayrshire, for instance, the local Church of Scotland Presbytery was informed that 'a partition is necessary to separate the schoolroom from the schoolmaster's house'.

The first act of Parliament which laid down details to which school houses had in future to conform was passed in 1803. It stated that:

> The school house should be commodious and suitable to the size and circumstances of the parish, but should not consist of more than two rooms, including the kitchen. The garden should contain at least one fourth of a Scots acre and be enclosed with such a fence as is generally used for such purposes in the district of the country in which it is situated.

The master was also to have the use of 'fields for the ordinary purposes of agriculture or pasturage, as near and convenient to the school dwelling house as conveniently may be'.

Just under seventy years later the Scottish Education Act of 1872 again laid down that the newly created school boards must provide an adequate school house for each of its headmasters. Most of the fine stone-built school houses, which are still a feature of most towns and villages throughout the country, date from the decade following this important act of Parliament, but there were soon protests from ratepayers about the additional cost involved, which increased the amount of local taxes which they had to pay as a result of providing this better standard of accommodation for the dominies. The Scotch Education Department in distant London reacted by sending the school boards a statement which read:

> Many think that the school buildings are too grand and question the economy or morality of erecting on credit houses which are so expensive, stately and imposing. There are undoubtedly too many instances of school boards having been vastly too extravagant for the pockets of the poor ratepayers.

Many of these school houses of the 1870s and 1880s still stand, good solid stone-built Victorian five- or even six-roomed villas, some even with bay windows, but scarcely 'expensive, stately and imposing', far less 'extravagant'. School houses went out of favour during the 1950s and 1960s when many headmasters regarded a tied house as a liability, especially as having a large mortgage on a private home was a way of obtaining tax relief. By the 1970s few education authorities any longer insisted on newly appointed heads, including an increasing number of women, who already owned family homes, taking up residence in the school house attached to their school or standing in its grounds. In the end most of the school houses were sold by the education authorities which owned them at the time of Scottish local government re-organisation following the Wheatley Report in 1975 to the sitting tenants, who were mainly headmasters or teachers, rather than go through the rigmarole of transferring them to the new unwieldy regions, which in their turn were abolished on 1 April 1995.

One dominie who was provided with a particularly impressive school house was the rector of Bathgate Academy, whose home originally occupied one of the wings of the Greek neo-classical building which accommodated the school. All too soon, however, as always seemed to be the case, more classroom space was required and the rector's home was requisitioned, a new school house of still impressive proportions being built instead on an adjoining site in the town's Marjoribanks Street in 1903.

Gillian Somerville, the daughter of Bathgate Academy's last rector before the school was sacrificed on the comprehensive altar, described life in the school house in a booklet published to mark the school's 150th anniversary in 1983. She wrote:

> The Rectory was a marvellous place for kids. With a garden full of trees and a house full of mysteries, what more could one ask for? From the outside it wasn't a picturesque house, but rather a massive square-set block of Calvinist severity. Through the inner front door you passed under the arch of a vestibule into the hall, large enough to hold an assembly. The darkly varnished wooden staircase swept upwards in a grand manner, carpeted, as was the hall in a rich cardinal red.
>
> The main public rooms opened off the hall. They were impressive spacious rooms. My father's study was a warm, comfortable, but dark room with a bay window looking out over the front lawn. My father's desk stood in the window. There were darkly varnished mantleshelves above the fireplace and the same wood lined the window bay. I searched in vain for secret panels.
>
> Access to my father's study was by grace and favour. When the furrows of, 'Do not disturb' deepened across his brow, indicating perhaps matters

of business, we had to keep out. Parents who came to see him were shown into this room. Here he prepared his texts for morning assembly. During the summer the large school time table would lie unfurled on the desk while he pondered all its permutations.

Next door to the study was the lounge, the grandest and least used room in the house. Upstairs were four sizeable bedrooms — one of which was turned into a playroom for us children — a boxroom and the bathroom with its original Edwardian fittings. The nether regions of the Rectory were nothing so stylish as the public rooms, but no less interesting. There was a large kitchen, where we normally ate. In one corner stood the Tayco boiler. High on one wall was a bell indicator. All or most of our predecessors had had live-in maids. Beyond the kitchen was the scullery, a cold place all year round with tall windows of frosted glass, through which the occasional cricket ball would come hurtling, spraying our high tea or the washing line with glass.

Above the kitchen was the maid's room and bathroom, which were reached by a flight of bare wooden stairs, the entrance hidden by a curtain. The maid's room looked out over the school playground. We took it over and played regularly, constructing shops and schools.

The garden, however, was the supreme delight. There was so much of it, a whole acre, and it was so varied. A broad straight drive led past the front door from the pillared gateway on the street. At the front was a large lawn bordered with short grassy slopes. Behind the house, beyond the drying green, were rows and rows of fruit trees and behind a high hedge was the wood. This was the real fantasy land, the wild wood of methaphor and far enough from the house for us to be able to play for hours undisturbed. With all the trees that there were and with its high enclosing wall, a favourite game was to travel from one end of the garden to the other without touching the ground. Those were the tomboy days of divided skirts before jeans were fashionable.

The rector's daughter ends on another sartorial note:

My brother, being not then at school spent the day watching the girls playing netball in the playground, but why they did so in their knickers was a source of great puzzlement to him. His own attempt to sally forth to the wall one day clad in his junior Y-fronts did not lead to the liberal disregard he had good reason to expect. These were happy years we spent at the Rectory. As children we had space and time and hours of unsupervised freedom. Above all we had privacy. My father was the thirteenth and last rector, facts of which, in spite of superstition, he was very proud. After us the Rectory was pulled down and a technical college now stands there in its place. I haven't been back to see. I don't want to be like Kim and when the jar is smashed be unable to remember the whole. I was very attached to the Rectory.

1. The dominie often had to cope with large classes.

2. Surrounded by his girl pupils this Bo'ness dominie was nicknamed 'Tarrybeard'.

PUBLIC SCHOOL, TORPHICHEN.

3. The stone-built, slate-roofed Torphichen Primary School, here described as Torphichen Public School, is typical of many small Scottish village schools. The school dates from the 18th century and on one of the walls is carved the burning bush symbol of the Church of Scotland. The Victorian classroom in the foreground is still in use, but the playground shed in front of which four pupils are seen playing has long since been demolished and replaced by the school assembly hall. Notice the rough state of the playground. At its peak the school had a roll of over two hundred pupils, including some twelve- to fourteen-year-olds not deemed clever enough to go to secondary school, who stayed on in what were known as the 'supplementary classes' or 'the advanced division'. Today the school role is around 70.

4. *Whipping a peerie, a spinning top, always made the walk to school seem shorter in the days when town streets were virtually deserted of traffic. It is interesting to note the boy's style of dress, with his school cap perched on top of his 'pudding basin' hair cut, his collarless shirt, knee breeches, thick home knitted stockings and 'tackitty' boots. It is interesting also to notice that he carries his school books in a satchel worn at his side and not in a leather school bag worn on his back as became the fashion in later years. Two girls are skipping in the backgrounds in front of the school playground shed.*

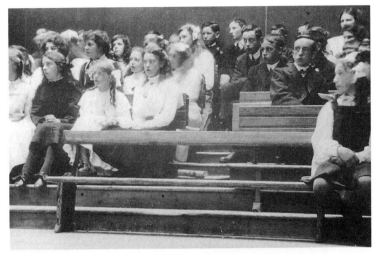

5. Pupils occupied the benches in the assembly hall at Bathgate Academy. The girl seated alone on the right wears a gym tunic. It is interesting to note the tiered seating, which was also found in many early Scottish classrooms, giving rise to the pun that pupils were always in 'tears', even on days when they were fortunate enough to escape the terrors of the tawse.

6. Bathgate Academy, with its classical façade, still stands in the town's Marjoribanks Street, but is now part of West Lothian College of Further Education, the school having moved to new premises on the outskirts of the town in 1967. It is, however, still on the steps in front of the old school that the John Newlands Oration is given, in tribute to its founder, on the first Friday evening every June by one of the school's distinguished former pupils.

7. *Bathgate Academy's most famous janitor, Billy Spokes, stands proudly on the steps of 'his school'. Before becoming the school's janitor, a position in Scottish schools which is derived from* Janus, *the Roman God who could look in both directions at the same time, Mr Spokes had served in the army and he brought his military style discipline into the playground, where he was never afraid of enforcing it with the aid of his short bamboo swagger cane, which he usually carried tucked at the ready under his arm. In addition to all of his caretaker duties, like many jannies in the years after the First World War, Mr Spokes was also entrusted with teaching P.T. Officially these letters stood for 'Physical Training', but according to the Academy's pupils who exercised under their janitor's eagle eye, they also meant 'Physical Torture', as he drilled them in winter in the school hall and in summer in the sloping playground in front of the building.*

8. Every schoolchild's dream came true in 1906 when fire swept through and gutted the north wing of Bathgate Academy. It is believed that the blaze started in one of the school's science laboratories, which were considered showpieces in their day. At its height the flames leapt high into the night sky and the entire roof caved in. The pupils who posed in the adjoining open field, while the photographer took this picture of the devastation, found their freedom short lived, because the Rector and his staff soon reorganised classes until the damaged classrooms could be rebuilt behind the Georgian style facade.

9. Pupils drilled with wooden staffs at this Midlothian primary school.

10. *A P.T., Pupil Teacher, posed with this class of boys when this class photograph was taken during the early 1900s. Most of the boys wear white Eton collars, named after the famous English public school.*

11. *Many local saddlers originally produced supple leather tawse when requested to do so by their town's dominies. Gradually certain saddlers like the Dicks of Lochgelly became famed for their expertise in producing punishment straps, which were particularly effective at administering the required sting, without leaving any tell tale marks on pupils hands and wrists and more importantly not doing any permanent harm. This Victorian view shows one of the Brownlee family talking to a customer in the doorway of their saddlery in Bathgate's George Street. The Brownlees became the major rivals to Dicks of Lochgelly in the production of school tawse during the 1970s and their range of straps was often advertised in the Educational Institute of Scotland's Journal. Teachers who placed orders were promised a prompt postal delivery of the firm's two- and three-thonged tawse, which were always manufactured from best quality horse hide and whose tails which administered the strokes were carefully hand finished to ensure no weal inflicting rough edges.*

JOHN J. DICK

SADDLER

150 MAIN STREET, LOCHGELLY, FIFE

PRICE LIST OF SCHOOL STRAPS

	Pence
21 in 2 Tail Light, Medium, Heavy and X. Heavy Weights	85
21 in. 3 Tail Light, Medium, Heavy and X. Heavy Weights	100
24 in. 2 Tail Light, Medium, Heavy and X. Heavy Weights	115
Miniature School Straps	25

All Prices include Postage and Packing

Terms : Cash with Order

Thanking You For Your Enquiry.

12. John J. Dick's price list for his firm's famous Lochgelly Specials, the most feared straps used by Scottish dominies. This list was issued in 1971 shortly after decimalisation of the coinage, thus even the price of the most expensive Lochgelly Heavy was quoted in pence. The firm later moved to Cowdenbeath.

13. *The School House, Torphichen, is typical of the hundreds of new residences for dominies built throughout Scotland following the 1872 Education Act. Built of sandstone and roofed with Scottish slates it consists of two floors with three public rooms on the ground level and three double bedrooms on the first floor. The kitchen on the ground floor had a bed recess built into the wall, where the maid slept and one of the bedroom's still has on the wall the bell which was pushed to summon her, when she was required. The house also has a spacious attic. The School House garden was linked directly to the school playground by a gate in the back wall.*

14. *These navy gym-knicker clad girls enjoyed a P.E. lesson in a West Lothian school in the late 1960s, but over ten years earlier at Turiff in Aberdeenshire in the autumn of 1957 this style of games outfit caused a bitter parental dispute with the local academy, which featured in the columns of the national press for several weeks. The stripes on the girls' knickers indicated to which school house they belonged. The girls in the picture enjoyed the freedom of doing physical education sessions bare foot, but this practice also caused several rows with parents in other parts of Britain and in 1996 led to a family of children in Yorkshire being excluded from school, because of their parents' refusal to allow them to participate in lessons without shoes* (Photo Jimmy Russel. Courtesy D.C. Thomson).

15. *Heads down, these pupils in a Scottish village school, concentrated on the work in their jotters. Notice the paper straws in the little third of a pint milk bottles, which were given out free of charge to all pupils at morning play time. On summer term days, the milk which was supplied by the Scottish Cooperative Wholesale Society was often luke warm by the time it was served, while on winter mornings it was often frozen and had to be thawed out on the heating pipes* (Photo Jimmy Russel. Courtesy D.C. Thomson).

16. An art lesson in a Scottish village school in 1969. The classroom lacked a running water supply and so water was fetched in jars from a sink in the toilets (Photo Jimmy Russel. Courtesy D.C. Thomson).

17. *The author, and his smartly uniformed pupils, pose in front of Linlithgow Primary School, as they receive* The Scotsman School Magazine *Award in 1986* (Photo Bob Wallace. Courtesy Linlithgowshire Journal and Gazette).

18. The author at his desk, the top of which is covered with a variety of school artefacts including a school brass bell, a school slate, ink well, wooden pointer and at the far end a black leather tawse. On a more cheerful note hanging on the far shelf are two iron girds, the metal hoops which pupils of former generations loved to trundle around the playground at playtime and lunchtimes, propelling them with iron handles known as cleeks. The bottom section of a sampler, so called because girl pupils in Victorian times had to complete one to show samples of all the stitches which they had learned, can be glimpsed on the wall behind the desk (Photo Courtesy D.C. Thomson).

19. *The author rings the school bell in front of the entrance to Torphichen Primary School, where he became Scotland's youngest dominie when he was appointed in 1969* (Photo Courtesy D.C. Thomson).

– 10 –
THE DOMINIE AT PLAY

'**G**oing home at four o'clock', is supposed to have been the Scottish schoolboy's classic response, when asked what he liked most about school.

Nine 'til four, was, however, not always the traditional school day for the dominie and his pupils. A nine o'clock start would in fact have been considered almost a holiday, because in the early religious schools lessons began as soon as the first service of the day was over and that could be as early as 4.30 a.m. Even after the Reformation in the middle of the 16th century the school day still tended to be governed by dawn and the coming of the first daylight, so that in the summer months a starting time of five o'clock was common.

Such an early start to lessons did not however mean that the dominie was free from lunchtime onwards to pursue his own interests, as were his Scandinavian and Continental counterparts. The Scottish school day was probably the longest in Europe, starting at five in the morning and not finishing until six at night, with two breaks from nine until ten for breakfast and from noon until two o'clock for lunch. To make matters worse, there was also school on Saturdays, but at least classes finished at 2 p.m.

This pattern continued into the sixteen hundreds but gradually, as the 17th century wore on, 5 a.m. was abandoned as the starting time and 6 a.m. became the accepted time for the dominie to toll the school bell to summon his pupils to their lessons. This shortening of the Scottish school day brought protests from the provosts and bailies in many towns that the resultant long lies would lead to laziness among the pupils, and the dominies were blamed for contributing to the current corruption which they insisted was already affecting the youth of the country.

Despite these protestations further concessions were on the way, starting with a move towards seven o'clock as the school opening time during the worst of the winter weather, then gradually this hour was accepted as the normal starting time throughout the whole year.

Nine o'clock is first mentioned in Edinburgh in 1696, when, in September of that year, as autumn gave way to the early signs of the return of winter, the magistrates of the city, noting 'that the High School is situated in a corner at some distance and that the inhabitants are unwilling to expose their tender children to the cold mornings, do order the masters to convene the school at nine a.m. from the first day of November to first March and to teach the scholars till twelve noon, that which they were in the use to teach in the mornings and the forenoon'.

Most other Scottish burghs, however, frowned on this official pandering to the bairns, and few followed the capital's civilized lead in giving up the early morning start to their parish schools, where the dominies continued to be expected to be at their desks at seven o'clock. Even at the start of the 1800s, masters and pupils at Elgin Academy still began lessons at 7 a.m. Over half a century later, during the 1860s, the Commissioners for Schools deplored the length of the Scottish school day, noting that at an average of nine hours it was almost double that expected of English schoolmasters and their pupils.

Magistrates and the elders of the kirk session in Scottish towns seem to have been determined to obtain every last ounce of work from their dominies and their pupils, sometimes even threatening to cancel holidays if school days were shortened. In West Lothian for instance, when Bathgate Academy Rector James Fairbairn appealed to the school's trustees to agree to Saturdays being left free from lessons, these worthy gentlemen only agreed after a great deal of argument, and then only to every second Saturday being a holiday, and even that only on condition that both the Christmas and Easter holidays be cancelled to make up for the lost school hours. Rector Fairbairn protested and was sufficiently forceful to persuade the Newland's Trustees, who governed his school, to reconsider the issue; and the holidays were restored before any of these days, so long looked forward to, were actually lost.

Battles over holidays were common in many burghs, with magistrates and sessions complaining about dominies granting far too many 'plays and pleasances to the bairns'. Two major holidays were generally allowed each year at some period during the summer months and at Christmas. The Christmas holidays were, however, often banned for religious reasons in the years following the Reformation and the coming of Protestantism. In Aberdeen, for instance, in 1575, the council banned the old Yule holidays because, 'inconveniences' were alleged to have occurred because the boys were out of school. When they heard that they had lost their Christmas break the boys marched in protest and the magistrates at their next meeting discussed 'the enormities' which they were alleged to have committed. The following year the same trouble flared again when the ban on the holidays was announced. This continued every year until 1581 when on St Stephen's Day, 26 December, the boys decided that instead of marching in their own time after school hours they would try a new tactic. They decided to stage a sit-in and occupied the classroom. The magistrates hurriedly convened an emergency meeting to decide what to do about 'the disordered bairns, who have taken the school, meaning to have the old privilege'. As the boys refused to leave their classroom and go home, the magistrates tried to reach a compromise by promising three days' holiday at the start of each school quarter, but the pupils refused to be bought off by this bribe. The Christmas battles therefore continued until in 1604 it is noted that 'the bairns have held the school by using swords, guns, pistols and other weapons and spuilzied poor folk of their gear — geese, fowls, peats and other vivaris, to their great hurt and scandal of the burgh and magistrates'.

In 1612 the magistrates blamed the schoolmasters for what had by then become an annual Christmas riot and declared that as the 'insubordination, where-of there is no such in any other burghs, is brought about by the slackness of the masters in chastising insolent scholars and that the said masters shall be answerable for all disorders committed at the superstitious time of Yule'.

Other councils continued to try to ban Christmas holidays as late as 1716, when the Dundee magistrates decided that New Year's Day should be a holiday instead.

Battles were also fought to secure summer holidays, and one of these midsummer affrays tragically ended in the death of an Edinburgh magistrate. The year was 1595 and on 15 September the scholars of the High School marched to the Council Chambers in the High Street and petitioned for a holiday, or 'privilege', as they described it. That year, however, their petition was refused and so they armed themselves and took possession of the school. Dominie Rollock tried in vain to gain entry to his own school and turned to the magistrates for support. They soon arrived and Bailie John MacMorran tried to force open the door. As he banged and shoved there was a loud report, 'and he was slane by the schot of ane pistol on the forehead, out of the scholl'. The boys were arrested and one of them was charged with the killing, but as he was a rich young gentleman with influential connections the matter was discreetly dropped before it reached court.

Exactly when the summer holidays should take place was also a matter of considerable debate, this time involving the dominies more than their pupils. In general, the holidays were taken later in the summer than the modern break from the beginning of July until mid August. In 1748 the rector of the grammar school in Ayr put forward the following argument for the summer holidays to begin earlier, preferably in June. He wrote:

> First, the month of May in this climate is generally cold, the fields wintry face and there is little abroad to entertain either the senses or imagination. Secondly, this is the month in which the birds build their nests and boys often run great hazards by being at liberty to stroll abroad in quest of them. Thirdly, several scholars for a good many years past have been in use to repair to Arran, or other distant places, for goat milk and seldom return till the Fair week, which happens on the last of June and would be more convenient for them that this time were taken from the vacation than from the usual time of attending school. Fourthly I have observed for a good many years past that any scholars from Carrick or Galloway do not come till some time after the June Fair and the parents usually speak with the masters to provide a place for lodging their children whom they send down some days after. Fifthly, Scotland in general seems to be so sensible of the force of one or other of the fore-going reasons that no school has its vacancy sooner than June and most of them later.

Dominies and their pupils also enjoyed several one-day holidays during the course of the year. One which both masters and boys looked forward to in particular was Shrove Tuesday, in February, which they called 'Fastern's E'en'. The reason was that this was the occasion for the annual school cock fights, which the dominie organised and from which he also benefited financially. In 1724 at Dumfries, the council decreed that, 'At Fastern's E'en, upon the day appointed for the cocks fighting in the school house, the under teacher shall keep the door and exact no more than twelve pennies Scots from each scholar for the benefit of bringing a cock to fight.'

The description of the school cock fights at Dumfries goes on to tell how they were always attended by 'gentlemen and persons of note'. The cockerels were carefully matched and the dominie stationed himself beside the blackboard to record the bets. Once all the bets had been placed the dominie gave the signal for the two birds to be released and as they slashed at each other and the blood and feathers flew, he acted as referee. As well as collecting all the profits from the bets and the money paid by both boys and adults for admission, the master also enjoyed the prerequisite of all the defeated runaway cockerels. They were called the 'fugies', meaning the fugitives, and their fate was to end in the dominie's cooking pot.

The money from the annual cock fights became such an accepted addition to the dominie's income that in 1755 it was taken into account when calculating the salaries of the assistant masters at the grammar school in St Andrews, 'the first receiving half of the money and the second, the other half'. In *The History of the Parish Schools of Scotland*, written in 1898 by the Revd Alexander Wright of Musselburgh near Edinburgh, it is stated that cock fighting continued in the schools until the beginning of that century, but increasingly this barbarous sport came in for criticism and in one case the campaign to abolish it was led by the schoolmaster. He was the dominie at Kinghorn, on the shores of the River Forth, and in 1767 he proposed to the town council that cock fighting should be abolished at his school and that two days' holiday, until then given at Shrove Tuesday, should in future be given instead at the beginning of March. Feelings were apparently divided on the subject, because the councillors decided to refer the matter of the cock fights to the kirk session. It was only after the elders on the session declared that they thought that cock fighting was not only 'improper', but 'inconsistent with humanity', that the dominie's appeal for its abolition was finally granted.

While gambling on the results of cock fighting was approved in many Scottish schools, the dominies always frowned upon any other gambling or betting by their pupils, and both playing cards and dice were forbidden both in the classrooms and playgrounds. In Dunbar in 1679, for instance, the councillors ordered 'the scholars to abstain in their games from cards and dice and playing with or for money'.

Playground supervision was a duty forced onto the dominies from a surprisingly early date. In 1655 the master of Jedburgh Grammar School was instructed to ensure 'that good order shall be kept among the scholars at play'. In 1671, when the councillors in Aberdeen heard that 'when the scholars get play, they have not only disturbances and outbreaks among themselves, but also with the old scholars', they ordered that 'the master or one of the doctors shall, at such times, always attend on the scholars, causing them to keep to the ordinary places of playing and to use such recreations as may not be prejudicial to themselves or their fellows'.

One reason why the early Scottish school authorities were so strict about playground supervision may have been that they actively encouraged the boys to bring their bows and arrows to school, because skilled young bowmen could make all the difference to the defence of a town in time of attack by an enemy. First mention of archery at a Scottish school comes in the sixteenth century. It is recorded that the boys at the school at Logie, Montrose, were taught 'how to handle the bow for archerie'. In Perth in 1624, the town council gave its blessing 'according to use and wont for the scholars to carry their bows and arrows as they go about the town'. Around the same period, the dominie of Glasgow Grammar School was reminded, according to the city's records, 'to ordain the scholars to prepare their bows for archery', while in Perth in 1624 the town council gave its blessing 'according to use and wont for the scholars to carry their bows aud arrows as they go about the town'. Around the same period the dominie of Glasgow Grammar school was reminded according to the city's Burgh Records, 'to ordain the scholars to prepare their bows for archery'.

Many other games, ranging from handball to snowballing were

banned from Scottish paygrounds, for the councils, sessions and dominies were always watchful to forbid any activity which might result in costly repairs. In May 1774, for instance, the council at Ayr forbade the handball 'as it does damage to the slates and windows'.

Three unusual sports were against the rules at Glasgow Grammar School. They are noted as 'French kylis, alie bowlis and glakis', but why pupils could even be fined as well as whipped for indulging in them must remain a mystery as no record remains of what was involved in these games.

Many games which were recorded as both permitted and popular in Scottish schools in the Commissioners' Report of 1868 are now also unfortunately forgotten. These included 'Smuggle the Keg', which was reported as being a favourite in the playground at Kirriemuir Seminary, and 'Cross Tig' and 'Scotch and English Jackson', both of which were mentioned in the return from Arbroath High.

Most schools reported marbles, or 'bools', or 'taws' as being particularly popular with the boys at certain times of the year, but what none of them explain is how pupils down through the ages knew exactly when the craze for marbles should give way to other olden-time favourites such as whipping tops, iron girds and leapfrog.

While they often tried to share the laddies' 'bools' and 'jarries', 'girds' and 'cleeks', the lassies seem always to have preferred bouncing balls, and 'cawing' ropes often to distinctively local rhymes and chants such as 'Poor Lady Lilbourne, died in the Gilburn', which was popular in the playground of Bo'ness schools right down to the 1930s, even although it recalled a celebrated suicide of three centuries earlier when the young wife of one of Oliver Cromwell's generals threw herself to herself to her death from the attic window of nearby Kinneil House. Probably the children's interest in this old tale was kept alive by the legend that on dark and stormy winter nights when gales sweep up the River Forth poor Lady Lilbourne returns to haunt her unhappy Scottish home.

Certainly Scottish youngsters have always loved games with an element of superstition and cruelty involved in them, and from Victorian times to the present day corners of playgrounds have served as prisoners' dens for characters as various as the celebrated body-snatchers Burke and Hare to the Daleks of Dr Who, while prisoner's base was specially mentioned by the Rector of Forres Academy in his report in 1868.

The most reported game of all then, as probably now, was football, which was recorded as the main playground occupation at Aberdeen Grammar, Arbroath High, Ayr Academy, Bathgate Academy, Caerlaverlock Hutton Hall, Crief Academy, Cupar Bell Baxter High, Dollar Institution, Dumfries Academy, Edinburgh High, Trinity College Glenalmond, Greenock Academy, Hamilton Academy , Inverness Royal Academy, Irvine Royal Academy, Kirkcudbright Academy, Lanark Burgh School, Leith High, Moffat Grammar, Newton Stewart Institute, John Neilson Institute in Paisley, Perth Academy and Madras College in St Andrews. Many of these schools also mentioned that their boys also played cricket during the summer term, but only in the form of informal playground knockabout games and not proper inter-school matches.

When it came to the dominie's own sporting activities many of them appear to have enjoyed a round of golf. It is the sport which poet Walter Wingate has his dominie enjoy in 'The Dominie's Happy Lot', when he included the lines, 'All Saturday at gowf tae play and aye the pay gaun on.' One fortunate dominie at Dalmeny, on the outskirts of Edinburgh near Queensferry, even enjoyed the privilege of being allowed to play free of charge on Lord Rosebery's private seaside links course on the shores of the River Forth. This was a right which the last dominie of the old school in Dalmeny, before classes transferred to modern new premises on the outskirts of the village, greatly appreciated and used to the full.

The same dominie was also an expert at bridge, and when promoted to a large new primary, in addition to organising lunchtime card sessions in the staff room, also took the time and trouble to initiate his older pupils to the game.

Other dominies are said to have preferred to use their intellectual powers to try to enhance their salaries by gambling on the horses even in the days when off-course betting in Scotland was strictly illegal. To circumvent this little difficulty dominies often enlisted the help of their jannies to place their bets with the local bookies' runners, making use of *nom de plumes* to conceal their identity. Thus it was that bookies often received betting lines from the likes of 'Chalkie', 'Jotter' and 'Tawse Tails', but were always far too discreet to question the true identity of the academic gamblers.

Even when off-course betting on horse and greyhound racing was made legal, betting shops were not the sophisticated places which they are nowadays, with live commentaries and large-screen television coverage of all the events. Major race meetings were, however, by this time regularly covered by BBC television just at around the same time as television programmes for schools were replacing school radio broadcasts. For one well-known West Lothian dominie the temptation to switch channels on his school's new 32-inch television became too much to resist, and on the afternoons of the Cheltenham Gold Cup or the Derby he became unavailable to both staff and pupils. He was thus ensconced in his darkened study with the curtains tightly drawn when there was an unwelcome, unexpected knock on his door. Knowing that all teachers and pupils knew far better than interupt his afternoon's 'work', he immediately sensed danger and swiftly removed his feet from the desk and reached across to the set to switch channels. He was just in time, as the county's new educational adviser made his entrance. Completely unflustered, the sporting dominie waved aside the clouds of smoke, and greeted his visitor with the words, 'My, these new schools' television programmes are really educational'.

By the time that television had been become an accepted classroom tool, several dominies had become football referees, no doubt finding their authoritarian role in the classroom helped them when they swapped their black gowns for black shirts on Saturday afternoons. Several went on to become football commentators on both radio and television, while one of the refereeing dominies achieved his own goal of becoming one of Her Majesty's Inspectors.

From the round ball to the oval one, no mention of sporting dominies could be complete without mention of the much-loved Borderer, Bill McLaren, whose pawkily-delivered weekend commentaries thrilled and amused audiences world wide, as much as his coaching delighted his pupils in his home town of Hawick on weekday afternoons.

Dominies at the microphone are, however, not a new phenonomen, because during the postwar years when ice hockey was a popular sport in Scotland because of the presence of several US servicemen who were excellent players, the principal radio commentator on the game was the Canadian born Rector of St Mary's Academy, Bathgate.

Swimming too has had its dominie sporting stars, from Portobello's famous Ned Barnie, who successfully swam the River Forth on several occasions, to Ian Black.

– 11 –
THE BALDIE HEIDIT MAISTER

'**O**or wee school's a good wee school, it's built o' stanes and plaister. Oor wee school's the best wee school, if it wisnae fur the maister.'

How fair this oft chanted playground rhyme's summing up of the relationship between bairns and their dominies might be was difficult to tell. For until comparatively recent times the old proverb, 'Children should be seen and not heard', definitely applied in Scottish schools, and pupils were not encouraged to express their personal opinions about their teachers.

That this was the case obviously suggests an authoritarian regime, and this view is certainly supported by the vast majority of Scots looking back on their school days. It is interesting to note, however, that many also end by saying that as they reached the older classes they perceived a more sympathetic caring figure beneath the stern black-gowned exterior; They recognise that their dominies were dedicated to achieving the best possible education for them and thank them for it.

Let us start first, however, with the dominie's physical appearance.

'He was a tall well made gentleman, who always dressed in dark trousers, frock coat, à la Gladstone, a stock tie and black silk top hat', wrote one former pupil whose schooldays began in Victorian times. Another notes:

Our dominie was the man in black. He always wore a thick black worsted three piece suit with a waist coat, the bottom button of which was always left undone. Over it he wore his black academic gown. We never saw him without his black, billowing gown and were convinced he even slept in it. Come summer or winter he always wore that gown and so not surprisingly we nicknamed him Dracula. His bite, however, came not from his teeth, but from his thick black tawse, which lived constantly across his left shoulder beneath his gown, except when it leapt out for use, like a living extension of his right arm. The black gown gave him the appearance of the executioner and added to the terror of his tawse and the intense pain of the pandies, which it doled out, before disappearing under its shroud to rest across his shoulder until it was next required, which was never long.

The black gowns and many dominies' habit of concealing their tawse beneath them, led another girl former pupil to write:

> In his gown he was like a conjurer and as bairns we were always intrigued about in which of its capacious folds his tawse lived like a real live snake. No matter how closely we watched, before and after each strapping, we could never decide where its lair was in the layers of his gown, but we knew full well that it was aye ready to spring out to sting our palms and bite the tips of our fingers.

Wearing a gown did, however, almost have a more painful ending for one Armadale dominie than for his pupils. For in the days when schoolrooms were heated by open coal fires the dominies always made certain their desks were as close as possible to the heat, but the West Lothian teacher came just too near, when one cold winter afternoon, to the delight of his pupils, the tails of his gown caught alight. As they watched entranced, one wee laddie at last shouted a warning. With great presence of mind the dominie dived below his gown, produced his ever ready tawse and proceeded to whip out the flames.

Whether his strap was henceforth more effective than ever, is not recorded, but many Scottish pupils were convinced that after they went home at night, their dominies utilised the dying embers of the day's fire to blacken the tips of the thongs of their tawse to harden them for the following morning's fray. Others insisted this same outcome was achieved by soaking the tawse taes in whisky, but some doubted the dominie would risk contaminating the flavour of his nightly dram for such a base purpose.

Legends of the 'belt', as children often called the tawse, obviously lingered in the minds of many former pupils, for they appear in many of their reminiscences from remarks such as 'Hold up was his constant command', to comments such as:

> 'The leather in his hands never wearied. Its thongs doled out their punishment with a regularity and impartiality, which would surprise modern doctrine. The smallest faults as well as major offences were dealt

with by inflicting corporal chastisement. Our dominies definitely believed in the wisdom of Solomon. To spare the rod is to spoil the child was their creed, or, as it was summed up in verse, 'Solomon said in accents mild, spare the rod and spoil the child: be he lad or be she maid, whip them and wallop them, Solomon said!'

Many former pupils, however, insist that they preferred the physical punishment which their dominies administered to the sting of some of their tongues. A former pupil of a Musselburgh school writes, 'He had a tongue that stung like a lash and sarcasm is a weapon which the schoolboy victim is ever slow to forget.' Although, as noted in the above verse, Scottish schools only very latterly in the 1970s officially differentiated between boys and girls when it came to corporal punishment; girls were for generations before then strapped by dominies if they judged their behaviour deserved it, and they appear to have suffered more from verbal chastisement if the number of their criticisms about sarcasm is a guide. 'At least it taught me the truth of the saying that sarcasm is the lowest form of wit', one girl ex-pupil of a Highland school recalls.

One day of the year when humour was appreciated on both sides of the desk in Scottish classrooms was 1 April, April Fools Day, or 'Hunt the Gowk' to give it its traditional title. There are many tales of the high jinks which both pupils and dominies got up to on this annual occasion. One Grangemouth dominie is remembered for sending one boy to the janitor for a long stand, while another in neighbouring Falkirk annually caught out one of his pupils by dispatching him to purchase a tin of tartan paint. Pupils on the other hand dared to try to catch the dominie out by hiding his chalk, substituting water for his ink, and even placing a drawing pin on the seat of his high chair. 'Huntigowks' in schools still happily take place, and not so many years ago a teacher at a West Lothian school arrived at her classroom to find her entire class had disappeared, only to discover them eventually all hidden below the tables in the library.

While in the past April Fools Day may have been the only day of the year when dominies willingly allowed their pupils to see the soft centre beneath their stern exterior, once a pupil reached the senior classes it appears from their school memories that many realised that their masters really had a much greater concern for their welfare than they had realised in the younger years. For instance, one pupil from Milne's Institute in Fochabers summed up his dominie by writing, 'he was an austere and forceful man, yet beneath his stern exterior beat a warm sympathetic heart'. Another former pupil of Fortrose Academy in the Black Isle described his dominie as, 'as great in heart as he was comely and powerful in frame'.

One of the last of the old-style dominies was the rector of a West Lothian senior secondary school during the 1950s. To use a modern term, he believed in corridor management, and his black-robed figure was a very visible deterrent to little first and second years. His manner was undoubtedly crusty and he thought nothing of picking up a miscreant in the playground by the scruff of the neck, tweaking the ear of an inattentive pupil in any classroom he cared to enter, or even walloping the occasional offending bottom. Yet no pupil would have thought of complaining, and by the fifth year they were the same pupils who appreciated being summoned to his home for extra tuition before the Highers and hopefully repaid him a little by mowing his lawn and trimming the verges. Even after they left his sixth year he followed the progress of each of his boys and girls and was always delighted when they came back to report their many successes. The motto of the school was the Latin *Sine Metu*, and it was indeed without fear that he did his job, and, like the captain of the sailing ship on its badge, was without doubt master of his school. Above the proscenium arch of the stage in the same school's assembly hall appeared the New Testament quotation, 'Get wisdom, get understanding; forget it not'; and that well summoned up his philosophy.

Mention of this Biblical quotation is a reminder of the important part which religion played in the day-to-day life of the dominie and his pupils. Each morning began with the command to bow heads and the communal saying of the Lord's Prayer. Jokes are often told of how incomprehensible the words of hymns and prayers were to the younger children, with one Edinburgh version of the 23rd psalm supposedly reading, 'In Parsons Green he leadeth me'.

On the subject of religion, according to one popular playground rhyme, the dominie had an ulterior motive for attending church. The pupils chanted, 'Our baldie heidit maister, he gangs to church on

Sunday, he prays the Lord to gie him strength to belt us weans on Monday.'

Another favourite playground chant, still sometimes heard at school camps and outdoor education centres, is: 'Build a bonfire, build a bonfire, put the heidie on the tap, Put the teachers roond aboot him and we'll burn the bloomin' lot!'

– 12 –
WHEN PARENTS HAD THEIR SAY

'Parents ! The worse thing children ever had!' one irate dominie is said to have snapped. His terse remark perhaps sums up the general view of dominies of past decades that like children, parents should be seen and not heard.

Nowadays, with Parent Teacher Associations, Parents' Nights and School Open Days so much in vogue, it is perhaps salutary to remember that until comparatively recent times mothers and fathers seldom came into contact with their children's teacher. Parental visits to school tended only to occur when their offspring had been very good, or very bad, and in the main consisted of attendance at end-of-term prize givings or irate meetings with the dominie concerning some misdeed and the disciplining of it.

'How many of the belt did you get today?', was a not infrequent question when children came home from school, and in general Scottish parents appear to have been strong supporters of school discipline even when, as it usually did, it involved physical punishment. 'Just you wait until you start school and you'll see what you'll get if you're bad', was another oft-heard threat to bairns before they even began the infant class. By tradition any child rash enough to complain at home about getting the tawse was liable to get another sound skelping from father or mother for daring to bring the family's good name into disrepute.

Very occasionally, however, parents would feel that a punishment had been unjust, or too severe, with tell-tale vivid red weals on their son's or daughter's wrists, as a result of a miss-aimed stroke, and would feel it their duty to come up to see the dominie about it. Usually dominies were adept at defusing such situations with calming words and excuses about how difficult it was to maintain discipline in large classes, how provocative the child had been, or how often the child had been allowed off in the past; and the parents would depart, satisfied that they had been listened to and been allowed to make their point. Parental respect for teachers was much greater, and in those days, long before children's rights had ever been heard of, the idea of taking a complaint further was rarely thought about.

The modern idea of rushing to the family lawyer to start a legal case simply did not exist. The idea of going to court was virtually unheard of, and the thought of taking a Scottish classroom matter to the European Court of Human Rights would have seemed so far fetched as to have been too farcical even for a St Trinian's comedy film script.

The other big difference between the rare parental confrontations with school authority in the past and the frequent disputes of modern times is that previously, as a result of the immediate use of corporal chastisement, the punishment was over and done with and could not be retracted. But now, children faced with the much slower alternatives of lines, punishment exercises or detention, know that if they are economical with the truth about why they have earned these sanctions, there is a good chance mothers and fathers will take their part and by coming up to school delay the evil hour when they have to complete them. Better still, by a slow war of attrition they may succeed in getting them off completely.

In the past too parental attitudes appear to have been very different, with some parents coming up to school to actually request the dominie to chastise their children for misdeeds committed at home. Most dominies appear to have backed the parent and whipped the child, but as long ago as 1595 one dominie took exception to this role of public executioner. He was Andrew Duncan, the dominie of the grammar school in Dundee, who, while defending the need for corporal punishment, wrote to parents protesting about being expected to carry out this painful duty for them. In his letter he states:

> Be diligent in correcting the youth. Do your part thereof! Indulgence leads to the gallows! Perhaps you would transfer this part of your duties to the masters of schools. But on what principle? Parents ! God has laid on you the charge of suppressing evil. The school is a place of intellectual exercise, not a place of execution. No wonder that so many, when they become their own masters, detest those studies that were rendered so bitter to their taste. Parents! you may do much to make your children like school and not regard it as a place of weeping and flagellation. Is it

not to be desired that they should of themselves prefer to attend school than lurk at home. But how is this to be effected, if indulgence prevails at home, while terror and the rod prevail in school?

On the other hand, the council in Dunbar in 1679 actually decreed that parents of pupils at the burgh's schools should inform the dominies of any acts of disobedience committed at home so that they could ensure they were adequately dealt with by admonishment in the first instance, but if stubbornly repeated by a properly administered whipping.

In past centuries, home, school and church were seen as the Holy Trinity in the upbringing of children, and there are records of Scottish children being soundly strapped on Monday mornings, either for failing to attend the kirk on Sundays or almost equally badly for not having listened intently enough to the minister's sermon to be able to answer the dominie's questions on it. In Aberdeen, for instance, in the year 1700, the council ordered the dominie to ensure that any pupils absent from church on Sunday or causing any disturbance during the lengthy service 'should be called to severe account on the Monday morning'.

Cleanliness was often held to be next to Godliness, and the dominie's criticism of the hygiene of any wean was sometimes the reason for a parental complaint. The most usual cause of parental wrath and indignation was if a child was sent home for allegedly harbouring nits, or worse still, actual live headlice in their hair. Headlice have always been and continue to be a major health problem in Scottish schools, to such an extent that in the past they gave rise to a saying still in common use in everyday language. The saying is 'to toe the line', and it came about because in Glasgow schools headlice were such a common hazard that to try to prevent the dominie being infected a circle was drawn on the floor around his desk beyond which pupils were forbidden to approach in the hope that the wee beasties would not be able to jump far enough to get into the dominie's hair. Unlike their country cousins, Glasgow's dominies at least had the support and backup of the city's army of 'Nitty Noras', as the school nurses who carried out the regular routine head inspections were nicknamed.

The embarrassing spectacle of head inspection is vividly portrayed in Glasgow's excellent education museum housed in the Charles Rennie MacIntosh-designed Scotland Street School in the former Gorbals district of the city. There too may be visited a whole range of classrooms furnished in the styles of various periods from Victorian times to the Second World War era of the 1940s. The dominie's room is also on display, with the man himself seated behind his desk, perhaps waiting for a parental visitation.

Next door, in the Scotland Street School, is a display of schoolwear ranging from a uniform blazer to the ubiquitous navy blue cotton Cherub gym knickers worn by generations of Scottish schoolgirls for physical education classes and games, all capable on occasion of provoking parental visits either because children were, or were not, required to wear a particular garment. Mostly, parental visits to school to complain about some aspect of school uniform appear to have concerned girls, including disputes about the colour of their stockings, or in more recent years tights, the length of schoolskirts, and latterly, whether or not they should be permitted to wear trousers.

One of the most publicised of Scottish school uniform disputes concerned whether girl pupils should wear shorts or gym knickers for physical education classes. It occurred in 1957 when an irate Aberdeenshire farmer complained to his local high school that no daughter of his was going to be seen running round the school playing field clad only in her blouse and knickers, as the P.E. teacher was demanding all the girls should do. Even when assured that the navy knickers which his fourteen-year-old daughter was being asked to wear were a recognised respectable item of sports wear, the farmer insisted his lassie was definitely not going to appear in her underwear. The school's gym teacher argued that for reasons of health and hygiene cotton gym knickers were an essential part of her girls' physical education outfit. The argument over the disputed knickers moved from the gymnasium and sports field to the rector's office, where, in these days before pupils' rights, the headmaster backed the teacher. The suggestion that the farmer's daughter be granted permission to wear navy shorts on top of her gym knickers was rejected, and so the school knickers row reached the papers. The debate on what constituted suitable sportswear raged for weeks in the Scottish press from broadsheets to tabloids, with the *Daily Record* even printing a large photograph of the offending garments. In the end a compromise was reached by the school excusing the lassie from the farm from taking P.E. classes until she was old enough to leave.

While parental visits to dominies' offices to complain about school uniform appear mainly to have concerned girl pupils, it has almost always been the opposite where hair styles are concerned, with fathers and mothers coming up to school to complain about their sons being sent home either because their locks were too long or too short. Perhaps because they were so often themselves 'baldie heedit', Scottish dominies appear to have become enraged about almost every new hair style from the crew cuts of the late 1950s to the colourful punk styles of the 1980s, and have been convinced that such hirsute deviance was a deadly danger to discipline.

In more recent years dominies' bans on boys wearing ear-rings have also provoked parental wrath. Generally, schools now enforce unisex rules, with heads' best chances of banning ear-rings and way-out hairstyles being to declare them a danger to health and safety in the gymnasium, science laboratories, craft and design and other practical classrooms.

Often, rather than broach the dominie in his den, Scottish parents have preferred to put pen to paper often with amusing results, such as the note which read:

> Please excuse our Jeannie for being absent yesterday because she caught a chill sledging down her granny's back.

Another famous note is said to have accompanied one wee laddie on his very first day at school in the infant classroom. It read:

> Hamish is a very nervous little boy. If he does anything wrong, just belt the child sitting next to him and you will have no more bother from him.

Back in the 1920s corporal punishment of a much more severe nature was the subject of a parental note to a Lanarkshire school. It stated:

> Excuse Sandy being absent for two days as he was away at Hamilton Burgh Court being birched and can only now once again sit down. I have the honour to be his mother.

Much more recently, during the 1980s, when the campaign to ban the belt was a hotly debated topic in Scottish schools, the campaign in West Lothian was led somewhat inappropriately by a mother called Mrs Spankie. Her campaign against corporal punishment led one of her supporters to send the following note to a Linlithgow headmaster:

James is never again to get the belt from either you or his teacher. Both his father and me object strongly to anyone touching him. We never smack him at home, unless in self defence.

The same Linlithgow dominie received another parental note about corporal punishment, this time from an irate father enquiring why his wee boy had been given two of the strap for talking. That afternoon the head sent a letter home explaining that the child had only been punished after repeated warnings from his teacher to be quiet, and that the boy must learn not to talk so much. To his surprise, the following morning he received a further note from the father. It read simply: 'If you think Ian talks too much, you should hear his mother!' And that was the last word on the subject.

Still on corporal punishment however. While the last story is true, the following one is definitely apocryphal. It concerns the father who came storming up to school to demand to know why his son had been belted during the religious education period. 'Jimmy was simply not paying attention', explained the headie. 'He couldn't tell his teacher who knocked down the Walls of Jericho.' 'Well if my son says he disnae ken, you can rest assured he had absolutely nothing whatsoever to dae wi' it. Oor Jimmy may be a wee vandal but one thing he's no and that's a liar. But if you promise no tae belt him again, I'll pay for the damage this time.'

Some parents, however, appear to have desired even more severe penalties for their children than were available in Scottish schools, even in the days when the belt held sway, if an excuse note received by a Stirlingshire primary school is to be believed. It read, 'Please execute Senga for being away a message.'

Health matters were the subject of many notes to dominies. One read, 'John could not come with his throat', while another explained, 'Colin was absent yesterday because he had the diria, direar, the runs!'

Girls' too had their health problems. 'Janet was off yesterday afternoon because she had to come home with her tummy.'

'Sheila has been absent because of her face. She has had it since she was wee and now the doctor says it is getting worse and spreading.'

'Bessie will be away from school for a few days. She came home on Monday with it and can't get rid of it at all.'

'Mary is absent because of her head. We are waiting to see what comes out of it.'

'Helen has been away from school because she has had the H.'

Another famous note stated, 'Peter was absent from school yesterday because his mother was washing his father George Bell.'

To conclude, even death could produce an amusing school note, as in the case of the following one, which announced, 'Please excuse Tom being kept at home yesterday because his grandmother died to oblige his mother, Mrs Gourley.'

Perhaps the final word should go, however, to the Scottish mother who addressed her note to 'The School Waster'.

– 13 –
WHEN THE WRITING ON THE BLACKBOARD SPELT DISMISSAL

During the late horrid and unnatural rebellion, the maister did encourage the scholars to write on their copies, 'Honour to Prince Charlie' and did even encourage them to make a bonfire in honour of the Pretender. He is therefore declared utterly unqualified as a teacher of youth and is hearby dismissed.

Thus ended the teaching career of the dominie of Fortrose Grammar School in the Black Isle in Ross and Cromarty. Dismissals of dominies were by no means uncommon, because parish ministers and the elders of the session, provosts and burgh magistrates and even parents all deemed it their solemn duty to keep a close watch on the maister's religion, politics, finances and especially morals, as well as the way he taught, disciplined and generally conducted his school.

One of the first masters to be deprived of his office because of his religious beliefs was Ninian Winzet, the dominie of Linlithgow Grammar School. At the time of the Reformation all school masters were required to sign, under pain of dismissal, the Confession of Faith. Winzet, who had had many long arguments with no less a figure in the church than John Knox himself, point blank refused to put his name to the document. His refusal caused considerable controversy, and John Spotswood, Church Superintendent of Lothian, hastened out from Edinburgh to the royal and ancient burgh. There, together with the minister at Linlithgow's famous St Michael's Kirk, the Revd Patrick Kenloquhy, he tackled Winzet about his stubborn adherence to the old Roman Catholic beliefs. For hours on end they argued fiercely, but 'despite diverse conferences to make him confess his errors', he remained 'obstinate', and so, finally, was deprived of his office. For Winzet, however, it proved a good move, because he emigrated to Germany where he went on to become Bishop of Ratisbon.

Religious persecution of dominies continued into the 17th century, when many lost their livings, because they supported the Covenanters. Once more, the dominie of Linlithgow's Grammar School was amongst those who suffered, when, in 1674, David Skeoch was 'removed from his office as master of the Grammar School, on account of his refusing to abstain from attending conventicles'. Again, however, it is good to note that dismissal from Linlithgow led on to better things, because only two years later, he accepted the post of Rector of the larger Paisley Grammar School, but only on condition that he 'may have security of trouble from superior persons'.

Back in Linlithgow the authorities never seemed to learn their lesson, for yet again they quarrelled with their dominie, Skeoch's replacement, who was the scholarly and celebrated James Kirkwood, whose Latin primer was used in schools throughout Scotland for almost two hundred years. Kirkwood was appointed in 1675. His pupils included the future Earl of Stair, and James Gardiner of Burnfoot, who became a colonel, and features in Sir Walter Scott's Waverley Novels. Kirkwood first came to prominence in local affairs outside of his schoolroom four years later, in June 1679, when, after the Battle of Bothwell Bridge, 1200 Covenanters were taken prisoner and on their forced march to punishment in Edinburgh, were lodged overnight in Linlithgow.

According to the session minutes of Linlithgow's St Michael's Kirk, the defeated Covenanters 'caused great scandal' as they entered the town at the West Port, because many of them were stark naked! So perturbed at this state of affairs was dominie Kirkwood, that, although he opposed their religious beliefs, he tried to provide as much help as he could. He went to the captain of the guards, Alexander Brown, and persuaded him to give him his regimental cane, as a symbol of safe conduct to the soldiers. He then went to where the prisoners were being held captive at the town's flesh market. Later he described his humanitarian actions in his own words:

> From three in the morning until ten in the forenoon, I alone stood on the Flesh Market wall and gave in over three hundred suits of clothes, and exceeding much meat and drink, not without hazard to my person,

being often like to follow the cord with which I let down the barrels to the prisoners, of whom many thereafter came back and thanked me heartily for the favour I had down them.

Where the lowly paid dominie obtained all these clothes and food to distribute is not explained, but later, during his dismissal proceedings, he used this incident as evidence of his unbiased nature.

Kirkwood's dismissal from the Grammar School at Linlithgow did not come about because of his intervention with the prisoners, but because of the complete change in the political scene, when the Bloodless Revolution of 1689 suddenly brought the Protestant William and Mary of Orange to the throne, and he suddenly found himself on the opposition side. Despite the fact that he was one of the best-known schoolmasters in Scotland, to his fury Kirkwood suddenly found himself commanded to appear before the Provost and magistrates to swear allegiance to the Protestant cause.

To make matters even worse for Kirkwood, the Provost was young Walter Stewart of Pardovan, who according to the enraged dominie, was 'a mere lad, scarce out of the schoolroom!' Now, from the heights of his position as Provost of the Royal and Ancient Burgh, Stewart demanded that Kirkwood attend Protestant services. Kirkwood refused to go to any Protestant church service and was consequently dismissed, but he had the last laugh, because he promptly published *The Twenty Seven Gods of Linlithgow,* in which he lampooned each and every one of his former employers in what became one of 17th-century Scotland's most famous satires. Kirkwood also went to court, where the legal wranglings went on for years, but eventually in 1712 the proceedings reached the Scottish Privy Council where the lords found in his favour and Linlithgow had to pay him damages and costly expenses to compensate, not just for his loss of his position, but also because they had forced him and his Dutch wife, Goletine, to leave the Linlithgow school house, as a result of which they had had to sell all of their fine Dutch furniture. In addition, Kirkwood's dismissal appears to have done him no harm career-wise as he went on to become dominie at Kelso. During his time at the Borders school, he was summoned to appear before a parliamentary commission appointed to inquire into the state of Scottish schools, and as a result of his evidence he was commissioned to produce a new Latin grammar book, which proved so popular that it continued to be used for over 150 years.

Another dominie whose dismissal became the talk of the country was John Cunningham, but his case did not have the happy ending which Kirkwood enjoyed. For Cunningham, who was the master of the school at Prestonpans on the south shore of the River Forth, was accused in a case of black magic and witchcraft, involving no less a person than the Scottish King, James VI, who in 1603 also went on to become James I of England under the Union of the Crowns.

Persistent rumours circulated through the little coastal town for several years that Cunningham led a double existence as respectable dominie by day, but as an infamous warlock by night. All of his pupils knew that his nickname was Dr Sin, but strangely it was not the bairns who had given him this sinister title, but their mothers and the other womenfolk of Prestonpans. Intriguingly, while none of the women would admit to having actually themselves participated in any of the dominie's extra-curricular lessons, all knew the intimate details of these spine-chilling night classes.

It was, for instance, alleged that at Hallowe'en 1590, as the skies darkened over Prestonpans and the October night was lit only by the ruddy glow of the fires of the town's salt pans, dominie Cunningham led a procession of no fewer than two hundred of his female followers down to the harbourside. The lessons which he was to teach the ladies that night, were, however, very different from those which he whipped into their sons and daughters with his tawse by day, for under cover of darkness he exchanged his role of God-fearing dominie for that of the Satan-worshipping Dr Sin. Once on the quayside, with his dominie's black cloak still swirling round him as the wind lashed the waters of the Forth into choppy waves, he supervised the embarkation of all of the women into a fleet of small boats. When all were on board, he joined them, standing high in the prow of the leading craft as it led the little fleet out of the harbour mouth and into the even more storm-tossed waters of the Forth. For on that All Hallow's Eve they were to voyage down the windswept firth all the way to North Berwick, where they had an appointment to meet no less a figure than the Devil himself.

Excitement ran high as the boats bobbed their way down the coast like apples in a Hallowe'en cauldron. The shrieks and laughter of the women could be heard from the shore as they emptied the flagons of ale and wine, which they had taken aboard with them to fortify themselves for their forthcoming assignation at the harbour-side parish kirk at North Berwick, where dominie Cunningham, alias Dr Sin, promised the De'il was awaiting their coming.

After landing at North Berwick, despite Cunningham's exhortations that they must make all possible haste to the church, the women of the coven began to dance and sing on the high harbour wall. The voyage from Prestonpans had already taken much longer than he had anticipated, so in the end he led them, still dancing and chanting, into the church, whose ruins still stand at the end of Shore Street. There, their noisy clamour was quickly stilled. For, waiting to greet them by the pulpit, was the black-clad figure of Auld Nick.

Today, historians believe that this terrifying apparition, 'with goat-like beard and flowing tail', was Francis Stewart, Earl of Bothwell, because he had the chance to gain the Scottish throne if James VI died childless, and an attempt to kill the monarch was to be the work of that dark night. First, however, the figure by the pulpit ranted and raved at the warlock Cunningham, and the women who he had brought, for their late arrival. Then, by the flickering light of the candles on the holy communion table, several of the women later described how in his horribly shrivelled hand he produced from beneath the folds of his black cloak, just like the one Cunningham wore by day in his classroom, a waxen doll, which was to represent King Jamie in the satanic rites which followed.

Wrapping the image in a piece of white linen, obtained, he declared, by one of the young serving wenches at the royal Palace of Holyrood, and which he assured Cunningham and his women had only recently been worn by his majesty, the black clad figure began piercing it with needles. Then Cunningham, and each of the women in turn, came forward, touched the wax doll and wished death upon the king.

It was, however, the death of dominie James Cunningham himself which resulted from the coven's North Berwick convention, because King James soon heard of the events. A convinced believer in the powers of witchcraft, the king ordered the interrogation of Cunningham's servants, and one of them, Agnes Sampson, provided him with the alleged truth of what had happened in the North Berwick parish kirk. That was all the evidence which King James required to quickly order the arrest of Cunningham, and to swiftly summon a witch trial to convene at the Tolbooth Jail in the shadow of the High Kirk of St Giles in Edinburgh's High Street, just up the Royal Mile from his residence at Holyrood.

Interestingly, the Earl of Bothwell did not even wait for the trial to begin, but left Scotland for the safety of exile in Italy. For John Cunningham, however, there was to be no escape. The king himself took charge of the proceedings in the thick stone-walled prison in Parliament Square, and with a torture chamber set up in an adjacent cell to remind witnesses of the black magic alleged to have been practised on that Hallowe'en night, there was no lack of evidence set before him and the lords who made up his commissioners.

It is claimed that it was at the trial of the Prestonpans dominie that the thumbscrews were used for the first time in Scotland, and under their terrible torture he confessed not only to his part in that black Satanic night at North Berwick, but also to a previous attempt on the king's life. This had happened on the night when James was sailing home from Denmark with his bride to be, the little Princess Anna. Well did James remember the fierce storm which had arisen as the royal vessel entered the Firth of Forth just at the point where, having finished the crossing of the North Sea, she should have been almost safely home to Scotland in the more sheltered waters of the river. Now King James knew why the lives of his future queen and himself had been put so terrifyingly at risk, as John Cunningham admitted that he had been responsible for the gale. As the iron thumbscrews bit deep and crushed his bones, he confessed that on that night he had ridden from Prestonpans to the neighbouring town of Tranent. There he had chased and caught a black cat. Flinging the terrified beast into a sack, which he had brought with him for the purpose, he whipped his horse, and, lighting his way by 'raising up four candles upon the horse's lugs and another candle upon the cane, which the man who was with him had in his hand, which gave sic licht as if it had been daylicht', they rode back to the shores of the Forth and there threw the cat into the waters of the river. As the beast drowned he admitted that he had called upon the Devil to whip up such a storm that the royal vessel sailing back to Scotland from the Danish court would be wrecked as she entered the Forth, and that, like the cat, both King James and his Princess Anna would be drowned below its waves.

As soon as the thumbscrews were released and the excruciating torment of the torture ceased, Cunningham retracted his confession. This news was quickly conveyed to the king, who had returned home to the palace at Holyrood. Furious, his majesty immediately rode back up to the Tolbooth and remained present while the schoolmaster was subjected to the severest forms of torture which the Edinburgh city executioner could devise. First, each of Cunningham's nails was torn off with pincers; then long needles were inserted one by one into each of his fingers and thrust in, right up to their hilts. When this failed to make the dominie repeat his previous confession, his legs were forced by the executioner into the dreaded iron boots, which slowly and excruciatingly crushed his flesh and bones. Despite this, Cunningham still refused to repeat his earlier confession. King James, however, then decided that this merely proved that the Devil had taken possession of Cunningham's heart, and so, inevitably, a verdict of guilty of witchcraft was returned. Cunningham was sentenced to be publicly executed by being burned at the stake. In January 1591, the Prestonpans schoolmaster paid the ultimate penalty. Watched by one of the largest crowds ever to attend an execution in the Scottish capital, Cunningham was dragged up to Castle Hill, where he was securely tied to a tall wooden stake, around which a bonfire had been built, already lit and smoking. Then, as the flames slowly spread and licked the body of the poor misguided Prestonpans' dominie, the executioner stood forward, and, placing a short cord round his neck, in traditional Scottish fashion, 'wirred', that is strangled the life out of him, before the fire reduced his remains to ashes.

Few dismissed dominies achieved the notoriety of John Cunningham, alias Dr Sin, whose career was chronicled in a best-selling penny pamphlet sold in the streets of London, most simply being removed from office because of inefficiency, incompetency, neglect or mismanagement. Such was the case almost exactly a century after Cunningham's execution, when in 1692, the dominie in Wigtown in south-west Scotland lost his post when it was alleged that 'the bairns were stravaiging and committing evill things by not being kept in the schule'.

A few years later, in 1713, it was not the pupils' truancy, but that of the master himself, which resulted in the sacking of George Glen, master of Paisley Grammar School, when he was dismissed 'partly for his non-attendance in the school and partly for his want of authority'.

Being too strict could, however, also cost dominies their jobs, because even in the days when 'spare the rod and spoil the child' was the accepted wisdom, local magistrates and session members differentiated between properly administered corporal punishment and thrashings which they deemed too severe, cruel or inappropriate, although their standards were different from those of the modern child-abuse-conscious age. No matter how many strokes of the tawse dominies deemed it necessary for their scholars to receive to keep them in line and learning diligently, they were expected to be sufficiently practised and skilled in their administration to ensure that they did not cause bruises, weals, or worst of all draw blood. The masters were also expected to restrict their chastisements of pupils to strokes of their straps on their fingers, palms of their hands, backs of their thighs, or buttocks. Blows to the head, or other indiscriminate lashes to other parts of the body, if reported to their employers, inevitably brought censure, and, if continued after a warning, ultimately resulted in dismissal. In 1767, John Hastie, rector of Campbeltown Grammar School was dismissed for, amongst other things, 'obstinately persevering in severe and improper methods of correcting the scholars, notwithstanding repeated injunctions to the contrary'. Mr Hastie took his case to court and was successful in the Court of Session in Edinburgh; but the Campbeltown council refused to reinstate him and appealed to the House of Lords. After arguments in the upper house, their lordships found in favour of the town and ruled that 'acts of cruel chastisement' justified the council in dismissing their dominie.

On the other side of the country John Howie, schoolmaster of Arbroath, was dismissed, 'for punishing his pupils in cruel ways', while in Glasgow, Hugh Muir, who was described as, 'the doctor of the Grammar School', was dismissed for, 'exercising too rigid and cruel methods of discipline'.

Sometimes, however, the magistrates were too late in dismissing a cruel dominie. Such was the case in Jedburgh in 1657, when the dominie was ordered 'to gie up the keys to the school', because, 'he had had a hand in the death of a bairn'. The best documented case of a dominie being found guilty of killing one of his pupils is that of Robert Carmichael, master of the school in Moffat. In 1699 he was dismissed from his post following the death of farmer's son, John Douglas, after a classroom strapping. Carmichael fled from the close-knit little Border community, but was later caught and arrested. At the trial which followed it was found proven,

> that he did three times severely and cruelly lash and whip the defunct upon the back and hips and in rage and fury did drag him with his hand upon head and back, with heavy and sore strokes and after he was out of his hands, the boy immediately died. It was likewise found proven that after the defunct's death, the side of his head was swelled and blue marks were thereupon with several marks of stripes from the small of his backs to his troughs (buttocks).

Surprisingly however, Carmichael was not found guilty of either murder or even manslaughter, because it was accepted that the thrashing had not been inflicted as a result of Carmichael's vindictive or cruel disposition, but as a result of his duty as schoolmaster to impose discipline. In the circumstances therefore, the magistrates ruled that Carmichael should escape the death penalty, but that instead he should receive a taste of his own medicine, because they ruled that the dominie,

> be taken from the Tolbooth of Edinburgh, by the hangman, under a sure guard, to the middle of the Lawnmarket and there lashed by seven severe stripes and then to be carried to the Fountain Well, to be severely lashed by five stripes and that thereafter the said Mr Robert Carmichael be banished furth of this kingdom, never to return thereto under all the highest pains.

Another dominie, who fell foul of the law, was brought to trial at Edinburgh's Tolbooth, and was finally sentenced to transportation was Henry Gudge of Borrowstounness, or Bo'ness, the old Forth seaport and mining town on the southern shore of the River Forth. Gudge was the master in charge of the school at the East Partings in the burgh's South Street. It was one of the largest schools in the town, but, despite what should have been a reasonable income, Gudge got deeply into debt. Most of the money he owed was due to be paid to local merchant and ship owner, John Anderson, the founder of Bo'ness Academy, who owned so much property in the town that he was often referred to as the 'Uncrowned King of Bo'ness'. Despite repeated warnings from Mr Anderson, Gudge was unable to repay his outstanding debts. Anderson therefore seized Gudge's home in Corbiehall. Evicted from his house, Gudge felt so bitter at Anderson's action that he decided to have his revenge, while at the same time making himself so rich that he would never have to teach again.

From the conversations of his pupils Gudge knew that Anderson paid one of the boys every Saturday morning to carry his week's profits to Falkirk, as there was, at this time, still no bank in Bo'ness. This, Gudge decided, was exactly the chance he was waiting for.

On the following Saturday morning, Gudge set our for Falkirk, leaving about half an hour before the boy always departed, but knowing that by walking slowly his pupil would soon catch up on him. This the boy did at the ideal place, where the last houses of Bo'ness gave way to the open fields at the Crawyet. The dominie immediately hailed his pupil and kept him talking as they walked on for about half a mile through the flat countryside bordering the shore of the River Forth. All the time Gudge had his eyes on the bulging money bag.

Suddenly the dominie pretended that he had seen a hare in one of the fields beside the Kinneil Woods. The boy, of course, could see nothing, and so Gudge immediately offered to hold the bag for a moment so that the lad could scramble through the hedge to see if the hare was still in sight. As soon as the boy was on the other side of the hedge Gudge ran off with all the money, and by the time the boy gave up his search for the imaginary hare, the schoolmaster was out of sight. After waiting for some time for his teacher to reappear, the full meaning of what had happened slowly dawned on the youth and he made his way to Bo'ness, terrified of what would happen when he reported the robbery to Mr Anderson.

The hue and cry was raised at once, but no trace could be found of the erring schoolmaster. A visit to the lodgings which he had been forced to take since being deprived of his house proved that he had taken all his possessions with him. With more than £300 at stake, a large sum indeed in those days, Mr Anderson decided to issue a reward of £25 for any information on the whereabouts of Henry Gudge. The reward posters were printed and published in Edinburgh, and it was there that a girl who had once attended Gudge's school in Bo'ness chanced to read one. This was to prove Gudge's undoing, for she recalled that only a few days before she had been surprised to see her former school teacher emerging rather unsteadily from a pub in Bristo Street. She had not spoken to him then, because, as she later explained, she had no love for the Bo'ness schoolmaster whose tawse had repeatedly struck her palms as she had struggled with the intricacies of reading; but after seeing the poster she was glad that she had learned her lessons, for thanks to Gudge's teaching she could clearly read and understand the details of the reward, which she wasted no time in claiming.

She ran to the High Street where she contacted the famous Victorian detective, McLevy, who was in charge of the investigation, and together they made their way to the pub where they found Gudge seated with a bottle of whisky before him. While the girl watched, McLevy summoned help and Gudge was soon arrested. When he was searched three ginger beer bottles were found in his coat pocket and each was crammed full of pound notes, which, when counted, came to a total of £190.

Henry Gudge was tried at the High Court and sentenced to be transported to Van Dieman's Land, as Tasmania was then called, for twenty years. Towards the end of the period he wrote one letter to a former friend in Bo'ness, stating that he hoped, having paid his penalty in full, to return to the town, but shortly afterwards he died in Australia in 1859.

Another Bo'ness teacher who was dismissed for breaking the law was Sarah Small who ran a dame school in Grangepans. Her crime was fighting in the street with her neighbour, Margaret Robertson. It must indeed have been a fight to keep Miss Small's pupils talking for days, for in evidence noted down in painstaking copperplate by the session clerk of Carriden Kirk Session, it is claimed that after Margaret Robertson had called the schoolmistress a 'witch thief', the teacher struck her hard in the face, then knocked her to the ground where she proceeded to administer the kind of trashing usually reserved for the worst of her pupils.

Another school teacher who was dismissed for fighting, this time with a fellow member of the profession, was the master of Peebles Grammar School, who, in 1712, was ordered to surrender the school keys after he had soundly beaten his young assistant following a quarrel over their respective rights to teach and discipline the pupils.

Short of physical violence, teachers were on occasions also dismissed for quarrelling among themselves. In 1795 for instance, the Rector of Campbeltown Grammar School and the English master were both dismissed after a dispute between them over who had the right to teach what.

Not only were Scottish schoolmasters expected to be above breaking the law or even letting pupils and parents see them quarrelling in public, but they were also expected to lead blameless private lives, for it was considered their duty to set an example for the rest of the community.

It is hardly surprising that not all dominies managed to complete their careers with their halos untarnished. Dismissals occurred not just for moral offences committed in the classroom, such as the case of the English master who was sacked from his post at Stirling Grammar School in 1665 for 'several base usages towards his scholars', but also for sins committed outside school hours. Two such cases occurred in Dunfermline. The dominie of the Grammar School, John Hart, was dismissed in 1703 'in respect that he had committed the crime of fornication'. Earlier, it is interesting to note that when another Dunfermline dominie, Robert Inglis, was found guilty of 'scandalous carriage with Elspeth Matheson' in the year 1639, the kirk Session of Dunfermline Abbey postponed his public rebuke until the Sunday before his departure from the town, as it would 'condemn and vilify him before his scholars'.

Across the other side of the River Forth from Dunfermline, at Queensferry, the Kirk Session was apparently not content with expecting their dominie to live a spotless life while in office, but even during his retirement, because in his book *The Education Act of 1696 in West Lothian*, Dr Andrew Bain records the sad case of retired dominie, widower, Isaac Wybar, who, two years after giving up his post was hauled before the session because of his relationship with one Isabel Daling, widow of Robert Murray. Poor old Wybar was accused of 'having a scandalous conversation' with Isabel, and of 'meeting her at unreasonable hours, in suspected places, to the scandal of many in the town'.

Wybar pleaded 'that he did intend marriage', but explained that his circumstances 'would not allow this' at the time. The Session ordered that if this was the case then 'he should abstain the company of the said Isabel Daling at all unreasonable hours, henceforth, or marry her before Candlemas or otherwise be reported to the Presbytery, as persons living in wickedness'.

In the end Wybar did marry Isabel, but the Session declared that they believed that his wedding certificate was a forgery and insisted that further investigations took place, before reluctantly allowing their former dominie to end his life in peace.

– 14 –
THE DOMINIE'S LOG

> The Log-book must be stoutly bound and contain not less than 300 ruled pages. It must be kept by the principal teacher, who is required to enter in it from time to time such events as the introduction of new books, apparatus, or courses of instruction, any plan of lessons approved by an inspector, visits of managers, absence, illness or failure of duty on the part of any of the school staff, or any special circumstances affecting the school, that may for the sake of future reference or for any other reason deserve to be recorded.

When the black leather bound school log-books were first introduced by the new Scotch Education Department in the 1870s, they may have seemed just another added chore to the already over-worked dominies. Instructions were instructions, however, and so bringing the log-book up to date became as routine a Friday afternoon task for the dominie as carefully filling in the new-fangled registers of attendance, which were also introduced during this period.

Thus today these immaculate copperplate tombs remain, providing us with a fascinatingly detailed glimpse of Scottish school life since compulsory state education was introduced by the Act of 1872, and especially since the beginning of the twentieth century. The Scotch Code, as it was known, stated that, 'No reflections or opinions of a general nature are to be entered in the log-book', but in many ways what the dominie chose to enter and how he chose to word his description of events does throw light on school life of the period.

The following extracts are all from the log-books of one primary school in a small market town in Central Scotland. They show how a succession of dominies recorded the day-to-day incidents which they judged important in their lives and those of their teachers and pupils throughout the first seventy-five years of the twentieth century.

It is interesting to note, for instance, in the first entry the name given to the holidays, and how this reflects the status of Christmas in Presbyterian Scotland at the start of the 1900s. In later items watch out for the deference to the royal family, the importance accorded to religious education, the prevalence of illness and disease, and the much greater effect of the weather on school life in former times. It is also interesting to note that, unlike local education authority schools in England and other parts of Great Britain, Scottish schools were never required to keep punishment registers giving details of the names and sex of children chastised, the number of strokes they received and whether they were administered to the palms of their hands, buttocks or the backs of their legs. Scottish dominies always maintained that once a boy or girl was belted, the punishment should be considered entirely over and done with, no written record being kept with which to reproach the culprit. This approach also appears to have been adopted in keeping the log-book, for mentions of instances of discipline are rare, and when they do occur they are entirely anonymous.

We open the dominie's log-book with his first entry at the beginning of the new century. Did he perhaps have a sense of making a little piece of history as he picked up his fountain pen and wrote:

8 January 1900. School re-opened today after the New Year holidays. Attendance very good.

16 February 1900. Attendance very low this week, partly owing to sickness and partly to stress of weather. Lessons according to the timetable.

2 March 1900. School visited today by members of the School Board.

24 May 1900. Tomorrow is a holiday in honour of the Queen's birthday.

1 June 1900. Attendance rather low this week owing to term removals.

19 July 1900. Today the children were examined in religious knowledge by Mr Jamieson, Member of the School Board.

20 July 1900. School closed today for the Summer Holidays.

24 Nov 1903. The pupils were photographed today.

27 Nov 1904. Needlework classes are to be discontinued after this week as an economy measure.

24 Nov 1904. Miss Roberts has telegraphed that she is not able to attend school today.

5 Feb 1905. Cookery lessons are suspended owing to the temporary disablement of the visiting teacher through a burning accident.

2 Oct 1905. The class taught by Mr X and today taken over by Miss Y had not had a geography lesson for the past four weeks, the time allowed for that subject having been given for other work. Mr X had previously been warned to pay careful attention to the division of time as approved by the H.M.I.s.

25 May 1906. Captain F___ visited school today and addressed the teachers on some points in the new drill syllabus.

20 July 1906. The annual inspection of the instruction of Religious Knowledge took place this morning, the examiners being the Revd ___ and two elders. An exhibition of physical drill was given in the hall.

5 June 1907. The local authority has ordered that the infant school be closed owing to a serious outbreak of measles.

1 Oct 1907. Many boys are absent at the potato gathering.

5 Nov 1907. The janitor is ill today and consequently the physical education lesson as marked in the time table is not given. The usual practice under the guidance of class teachers is however carried on.

24 May 1908. Empire Day. Today a Union Jack sent by the children of Australia to the children of the town was unfurled by Lady C. The children of all schools in the burgh assembled in the playground to witness the ceremony.

3 Sept 1909. The abolition of slates in the school has had a salutary effect on the neatness of exercises in writing.

10 May 1910. Today at the Cross was made the proclamation of the accession of his Majesty George V. The school children marched in procession to witness the ceremony, after which they sang the National Anthem. They were granted a half day holiday.

15 July 1910. 342 pupils are absent today, the cause being a fair in the neighbouring town.

18 July 1910. Dealt with the boys and girls who played truant on Friday.

10 July 1911. In connection with the new medical inspection of school children, the nurses for the county attended today and weighed and measured pupils, who are to be seen by the doctor next week.

26 June 1911. On Coronation Day all the school children of the parish marched to the park where they received commemorative mugs from the Marquis and were treated to refreshments.

19 Oct 1911. Mr X's composition and dictation exercise books appear to require more careful attention from him than they have been receiving. Every mistake in spelling should be marked and common shortcomings in writing should be pointed out both on the book and on the blackboard.

3 July 1914. Mr C called today and discussed arrangements for carrying out his proposed treat to the children on the day of the King's visit on 11th inst.

10 July 1914. King and Queen visited the town. In their honour, the children were presented with medals, the gift of Colonel C, with illuminated copies of Lord Rosebery's address to the children of Scotland, issued on the occasion of the sex-centenary of Bannockburn.

1 Sept 1914. School re-opened. Mr C Assistant Master is on duty with the Territorials. The drill instructor and janitor is also on duty with the Territorials.

13 March 1915. Exceptionally heavy snow has prevented many people reaching school. Morning attendance cancelled, school dismissed.

10 Feb 1916. Lecturer from Band of Hope visited school and delivered lecture on the evils of alcohol.

4 June 1916. A list of 33 pupils, whose attendance has been unsatisfactory during past months was sent to the clerk of the Board of Education.

10 Dec 1917. Pupils who may qualify in June have been placed in two classes of 40 each.

1 Feb 1918. Attendance is unsatisfactory. Messages is a very common excuse. There appear to be long detentions in shops owing to difficulties about food distribution.

16 Oct 1918. Influenza is very prevalent having been brought to the district by soldiers and sailors home on leave. Three teachers and 447 pupils absent. School Board by order of the Medical Authority closed the school this afternoon in order to prevent the spread of flu. School to remain closed until the epidemic passes.

2 Dec 1918. It was found today that of 43 pupils present in Mr X's class, 20 had not paper or other covers put on their readers. The rule that

books must be covered having been in force for some years and teachers having had the authority's regulations brought under their notice fully a month ago Mr X's attention has again been called to the matter, with a request that he will see that such rules are carefully observed in future.

12 March 1919. The janitor and drill instructor returned from war service. He takes charge of boys of the senior division. The girls receive instruction at the same time from the class teachers.

19 March 1920. Diphtheria and scarlet fever reported this week.

28 May 1920. Attendance has fallen due to sickness caused by vaccination.

4 June 1920. Many pupils still absent due to the effects of vaccination.

21 June 1920. Two teachers absent as they are in quarantine, a case of diphtheria having occurred in the house, where they lodge.

29 April 1921. Under the authorities scheme for feeding necessitous children forty-one have been enrolled and are now receiving two meals per day.

14 July 1921. Prizes for attendance were awarded to all pupils of the infant classes, who had made 98% of the possible attendance and to pupils of junior and senior division, who had 99% of the same attendance. In the supplementary division two merit prizes were awarded.

28 Sept 1921. Miss A. Instructress in drill called to take part in the work from 11.30 to 12. Miss A agreed to write to Captain ___ as to another period as the hour above is not on our timetable for drill.

3 Oct 1921. Following a fine morning, rain fell heavily from 10 o'clock and continued throughout the mid-day interval. The pupils being quite unprovided with overcoats, it was decided to carry on until 1.10 p.m. and mark two openings.

5 Oct 1921. Frank Bostock's Circus visited town. More than half the pupils intimated to their teachers that their parents desired to take them or send them to the afternoon performance at 3 p.m. In these circumstances it was decided after consultation with the Chairman of the School Management Committee to continue the work of the school until 1.30 p.m. and mark two attendances.

27 April 1922. Owing to an unfortunate breakdown of a motor car, W.N. was unable to reach school yesterday, but took up duty today.

15 Nov 1922. Dr. H. called today to examine some children whose parents had applied for relief in the form of boots.

20 Nov 1922. Some absences are due to lack of boots.

29 Feb 1924, Gallery in the baby room of infant school has been removed.

20 March 1925. M.O.H. visited school and took I.Q. of four pupils.

14 April 1926. Books to the value of £5 received from the Education Authority for use in the senior library.

26 April 1926. No temporary assistant is available in place of Miss A. The smarter half of her class has been added to Senior One and the other to Junior 2a.

9 June 1927. Today is a holiday on the occasion of the County Sports.

10 Nov 1928. Fire Drill was conducted. The R.C. boys in the workshop took part. The rehearsal was quite satisfactory.

11 Nov 1929. Armistice Day was observed at 11 a.m.

10 June 1931. Had to visit Miss P's class to chastise several boys and girls. Later in the afternoon Miss P came to my room and admitted the class had her beaten. Arranged for a change of duties.

25 Nov 1932. The discipline in Miss S's class called for my serious attention.

7 Feb 1934. Fire drill very smartly performed. School cleared in 65 sec.

18 Dec 1934. Fire drill. All pupils clear in a most orderly manner and within 50 sec.

3 May 1935. In celebration and commemoration of the Silver Jubilee of the accession to the throne of King George V, the children each received a box of chocolates and a medal provided by the Town Council.

6 May 1935. By order of the King this day was observed as a holiday in celebration of the Silver Jubilee.

7 May 1935. By authority of the Education Committee and with the approval of the Department all children attended a free cinematograph entertainment in the town hall, as part of the Jubilee Celebrations organised by the Town Council.

18 Dec 1935. Miss P. and the staff of the infant department held a Parent's Day. Between 70 and 80 mothers were present and saw the children at work.

28 Jan 1936. On this national day of mourning the funeral of his late Majesty, George V, the school was closed in reverent respect.

12 June 1936. Results of Control Examination reached us today.

26 June 1936. Pupils attended exhibition of cinematograph films about the care of teeth.

1 July 1936. Senior pupils were privileged to see the ceremony of welcome extended by the Provost, Magistrates and Councillors for the Sheik of Bahrain.

28 April 1937. Dr ___ visited school this afternoon in order to examine a pupil in Infant I. This pupil is resident in the Poor House and has given so much trouble to the Infant Mistress that I had to report him to the Governor, who arranged this examination. Dr ___ decided that he should be withdrawn.

11 May 1936. Miss P. was absent today travelling to London to see the Coronation procession. A flag staff has been erected in the playground. This afternoon at 3 p.m. a little ceremony of unfurling the Union Jack, given by the Education Committee was carried through and the flag hoisted. The children were arranged around the new flag staff, those in uniform, Guides, Brownies, Boys Brigade etc. being placed together as a saluting party. As a souvenir of the Coronation, books were presented to the pupils. School was dismissed at 3 p.m. for three days holiday to mark the celebration.

9 June 1937. Scholars to the number 166 accompanied by 13 teachers and the janitor paid a visit to the Empire Exhibition in Glasgow. The journey was made by special train to Bellahouston Park Station. The return journey left Bellahouston at 4 p.m. Two pupils failed to turn up at the station, having got separated from their parties, but they were taken in hand by the police, who had them sent home by a later train. (The day unfortunately was one of continuous rain, but the children made light of this inconvenience and had a good round of sight seeing. The rest of the school was granted a holiday.)

20 Sept 1937. Dr ___ called at the school clinic this morning to investigate several cases of rash upon pupils. She diagnosed this as a species of scabies and sent home the children affected. She stayed to examine all other pupils. Books and apparatus used by the infected children are being destroyed.

29 Sept 1938. Pupils were fitted with gas masks.

11 Nov 1938. Remembrance Day was marked by a brief service and pupils observed a two minute silence at the 11th hour. (Poppy day raised £2 17s 9½d)

1 Feb 1939. Under evacuation in preparation in this district the teachers have been engaged to make a survey of the available accommodation, 8 staff have had this work apportioned to them and to enable them to get it done as quickly as possible, the school was closed for the afternoon, two attendances being marked.

2 Feb 1939. Same procedure as yesterday.

3 Feb 1939. Same procedure as yesterday.

23 May 1939. Mr S. was released from teaching from 20 to 30 June to allow him to assist in the advance party work in connection with the camp schedule for school children.

5 June 1939. Teachers watched a demonstration of physical training by continental experts.

5 July 1939. This afternoon an inspection of respirators was carried out. It was found that in 36 cases a change to a larger size was necessary.

Sept 1939. School was to have re-opened on Tuesday 5 September but Britain declared war on Germany on Sunday 3 September and since this has been classified as a neutral area, intimation was received that the school would not be opened until provision had been made for the children in the event of an air raid.

8 Sept 1939. Teachers were all in attendance at the Academy to help with the billeting of evacuees, who were expected to arrive from the cities, but none came.

15 Sept 1939. School still closed, but teachers met to consider what might be done to occupy the children's time during the day and effect some control over their activities. It was decided that all the teachers should organize visits and excursions in the immediate neighbourhood of the town for all classes from the Primary Department. After a few days experience of this, it was felt that something more ought to be attempted with the object of trying to ensure that the attainment in English and Arithmetic reached before the summer holidays might be maintained, A general scheme was evolved, but the teachers undertook to supplement the general arrangements by activities for which they individually found facilities. The general plan was for each

teacher to issue assignments of work to the class to be done at home. A week's assignments were arranged at a time. For this purpose each class was divided into groups of 5 or so with a group leader. The duty of the leader is to distribute the assignments to the members of the group and to collect and deliver to the teacher the written exercises. Where such is possible the teacher on returning the corrected work sends by the leader a message to those who need attention drawn to errors, to visit her at her home. There is no doubt about the faithfulness of the teachers' service and of the response on the part of many of the pupils, but the voluntary character of the work has afforded for some a sufficient excuse for the minimum effort.

The teachers of the Infant Department have gone on peripatetic duty. Several mothers have generously given a room in their homes for small groups gathered in the immediate neighbourhood. A short lesson is given by the teacher, who then passes on to another area of the town. There has been an excellent response from children and mothers and very good work is being done.

12 Oct 1939. Today the teachers began the work of writing Ration Books under the direction of the County Food Controller in the County Buildings. Altogether 11,006 books were written.

6 Nov 1939. Pupils returned to school today on the order of the Education Committee. Five air raid shelters are being erected in the playground.

14 March 1940. The school was closed to permit teachers making a survey of available accommodation for the expected evacuees to expedite the work.

15 March 1940. School again closed to allow survey to be completed.

26 June 1940. Last night the first serious air raid occurred. There was noticeable some degree of excitement among pupils today. Many showed signs of weariness as if having been disturbed in sleep last night.

3 Sept 1940. School re-opened today, the first anniversary of the outbreak of hostilities. Re-arrangement of classes in the air raid shelter in the playground took place. Teachers have been instructed to take books with them so that lessons may continue during air raids.

24 Jan 1941. An 'Alert' sounded today at 2.25 p.m. The pupils took shelter. Were in these places for nearly an hour.

13 Feb 1941. An 'Alert' sounded today at mid-day. The children went to the shelter, where they remained until the 'All-clear' came, twenty-five minutes later. Thereafter owing to bad weather the school closed at 1.30 p.m., a double attendance being marked.

13 March 1941. An air-raid warning sounded at 9 p.m. last night and the 'all clear' signal was not given until nearly 6 this morning. Many of the children were out of bed all night and did not appear at school until after nine o'clock. School was dismissed at 3 p.m.

21 April 1941. War Weapons Week opened in the county today. First days's drawings in the school amounted to £100 3s od.

22 April 1941. Dr R. today began the administration of the second inoculation for Diphtheria. 95% of pupils accepted the treatment.

24 April 1941. A number of pupils are absent from school today suffering from the effects of Diphtheria inoculations.

28 April 1941. This afternoon a number of the teachers were required to go out to make a survey of available accommodation for families, who may be bombed out of their homes. By authority of the Director of Education the school closed and a double attendance marked.

2 Sept 1941. By consent of the Director of Education the new entrants are in attendance for a half day only. This arrangement is temporary, pending the Education Committee's decision about the staffing shortage.

22 Jan 1942. The heaviest snow fall experienced in this district for many years made travelling very difficult for large numbers of pupils. The attendance fell to about half the roll. In consequence the school was closed for the afternoon a double attendance being marked.

23 Jan 1942. Again the weather was so bad and the attendance so poor, that school was closed at 1.15 and a double attendance marked.

26 Jan 1942. Snow again forced school to close at 1.15. A double attendance was marked.

3 Feb 1942. On account of the very inclement snowy weather school was again closed at 1.15 and a double attendance marked.

4 Feb 1942. I.Q. of Qualifying candidates was tested today from 10.15 to 11 a.m.

10 Feb 1942. Owing to very bad weather school was closed at 1.15 and a double marked.

6 March 1942. Owing to a severe snow storm, attendance was very poor and school was closed at 1.15, a double attendance being marked.

2 April 1942. The school dentist called to examine and treat the new evacuee children, who are to begin attending this school following the Easter holidays, which begin tomorrow.

20 April 1942. School re-opened after the Easter Holidays. Mrs C took up duty as temporary evacuee teacher.

2 May 1942. The attendance of children in the infant department has fallen considerably owing to an outbreak of measles.

6 May 1942. The Qualifying Examination was carried through today. 42 candidates sat the tests under the supervision of Bailie ___ and Councillor ___.

29 May 1942. An extra drive for Savings in a Warship Week resulted in a sum of £188 17s 6d being raised. Contributions numbered 265 giving an average for the school of 8/-.

3 Sept 1942. A new evacuee teacher took up duty. In accordance with the King's request that this day be made a Day of Prayer a short religious service was conducted by the Headmaster in the school hall. The Infants listened to the broadcast service at 11 a.m.

10 Sept 1942. R___ T___ having been accepted as a junior student, began attendance for teaching practice this afternoon. Her times are to be Monday and Thursday afternoons giving a total of 3 hours service per week.

12 Oct 1942. A start was made today with the dinner Scheme. 184 dinners were ordered. Only 164 helpings of first course were provided. The dinners were served in two groups, Infants and Primary 1 and 2 at 12.13 and the others at 12.45. Three servers were employed. The meal was carried through in an orderly manner. A surprising number of the pupils used the cutlery (knife, fork and a spoon) easily and cleanly.

21 Oct 1942. Miss ___ is absent today having racked the muscles of her back carrying dinner containers.

29 Oct 1942. Intimation has been received from the Town Clerk of the decision of the Town Council to make an annual grant of £1 10s towards prizes for the dux boy and girl. The Clerk stressed that the Councillors did not want to encourage the idea of a prize of large

pecuniary value, but rather to give something as a token of distinction to the best workers in the school.

13 Nov 1942. School closed at 3 p.m. to allow teachers to go to the Academy to meet the Moderator of the Church of Scotland.

18 Nov 1942. Free vaccination has been offered to all this week as a precaution against small pox, which has made its appearance in Edinburgh. Most of the children have been done and the reactions in many cases have been so severe that the attendance has been severely affected.

23 Nov 1942. Mr King from the Scottish Band of Hope addressed the pupils on temperance.

17 Dec 1942. H.M.I. ___ visited the school. He complained about the seeming lack of ventilation in the boys' lavatories. He recommended that these should be washed out by the janitor twice a day. He also suggested the employment of bigger boys as attendants in these places.

1 April 1943. Practice in air raid shelters this afternoon went very smoothly.

5 May 1943. The Qualifying Examination was held today.

23 May 1943. A model bomber was raffled today in aid of Wings for Victory Week and realised the sum of £5 0s 0d.

29 Sept 1943. P.T. Supervisor called at the school today with samples of soles which might be utilised during drill lessons.

13 Oct 1943. School closed at noon today because of Lady Baden-Powell's visit to the county to inspect the Girl Guides.

8 Nov 1943. 'Raise The Standard' fortnight ended today. £251 3s 6d was the sum realised and 27 new members were enrolled. Attendance throughout the school is very bad owing to a great number of the pupils having influenza cold.

7 Sept 1944. The senior pupils were addressed today by a spokesman for the Ministry of Supply and by an airman, on the need for and uses of books of all kinds in war time. A 'Book Drive' is in progress, but the response is not promising.

23 October 1944. Two footballs delivered today about mid-day, disappeared between 3 and 4 p.m. and no clue has so far been found. The matter is in the hands of the police.

24 Oct 1944. Mrs P___, being a farmer's wife stayed off to help with the threshing.

27 Oct 1944. Amount collected for the Huts and Canteens, £2 4s 7d.

15 Dec 1944. 24 of the evacuees returned home today.

23 Feb 1945. So many of the pupils asked away to attend a touring pantomime that we closed at 3.30.

9 March 1945. A party of soldiers arrived here this morning and set up a wireless station in the playground.

8 May 1945. In accordance with instructions from the Director of Education and its obedience to a national order conveyed by broadcast, when the Prime Minister announced the unconditional surrender of Germany, the school remained closed on 8th, 9th and 10th May.

10 May 1945. County Architect called about repairs to the tarmacadam not carried out during the hostilities. I drew his attention to the fact that there is no drinking fountain available to the girls in their playground.

Cheque received today for £51 2s 0d to be distributed in any way deemed suitable for increasing share in the Victory Celebrations, on 8 June.

6 June 1945. Before closing this afternoon, pupils were assembled in the hall and a short service in thankfulness for victory was held. On dismissal each child was given a card containing the King's Victory Message to the children of Great Britain. Announcement was also made of the arrangements for the outing on the afternoon of the 7th which has been declared a Victory Holiday by the Education Committee.

7 June 1945. This afternoon the whole school went in ten buses on an outing, which is the way in which the Headmaster chose to spend the money granted by the Education Authority to celebrate our victory.

19 Sept 1945. Cheque for 19/3 received in payment for 77 lbs of rose hips, collected by pupils.

2 Oct 1945. Miss L___ is absent today with a sore throat. I myself took her class and can confirm the opinion of every teacher who has had them, that they are restless and inattentive.

26 Oct 1945. Special Savings Drive for Thanks Giving Week produced £210 10s 6d.

11 May 1946. School closed for the afternoon to allow pupils to compete in the District Sports.

12 May 1946. School closed in the afternoon for football and netball competitions.

23 Oct 1946. The Infant Mistress issued invitations to parents of children in the infant department to visit the school and see the children at work. A large number of mothers accepted and spent the time in the classroom while ordinary work was going on. A collection was taken the money to be used for renewal of percussion band instruments. The amount collected was £5 0s 1d.

15 Nov 1946. For the first time a school bus is to be provided to convey children from the country areas.

3 March 1947. 'Bird Man' from the BBC Children's Hour spoke to senior pupils when he visited school today.

16 April 1947. Complaint was made today about the dusty state of the seats and desks. Some pupils were disinclined to sit down. I sent for the cleaner concerned and turned the children into the playground while the room was dusted. This is a most inefficient cleaner.

23 May 1947. Nothing unusual to report.

26 June 1947. Pupils went on excursions of an educational nature.

2 July 1947. Boy Scouts practised in the hall. They received instruction in the Scottish country dance which they are to do at the World Jamboree.

2 Sept 1947. A speech therapist attended for the first time today. Several pupils were found to be without defect. Their trouble is slovenliness.

3 Feb 1948. A strike of bus drivers prevented some pupils and 3 teachers from reaching school.

8 March 1948. The telephone was installed today in the Headmaster's room.

21 March 1948. Electricians completed the job of installing electric light in the primary department and the plumber plugged up the gas pipes which are no longer required.

26 May 1948. To mark the Royal Silver Wedding pupils were granted a holiday.

24 Jan 1949. Janitor roused me at 7.30 this morning to report that the school had been entered during the night. Two windows were broken and a large hole was showing in the ceiling of classroom 3. It was later discovered that a gas pipe had been broken and that the gas was alight. The police were called.

30 March 1949. Pupils were allowed to leave school at 3 p.m. to attend a Punch and Judy Show in the Town Hall.

16 May 1949. Infant Mistress absent. Former Infant Mistress has come in voluntarily to take her place.

20 March 1950. Pupils were given talks by police to stress the need for road safety.

3 May 1950. Rota system introduced to ensure that a teacher is always on duty to supervise the 160 children who take school lunches.

22 Sept 1950. A road crossing marshal is to be appointed because of the steady increase in traffic on roads around the school.

11 Nov 1950. Over 80 seven year olds were mentally tested.

5 Dec 1950. Letter from Director of Education was received stating that the newly appointed road crossing marshal would report to the Headmaster to collect portable sign. No street marshal appeared.

14 March 1951. Qualifying examination was carried out today. School closed at the end of the examination at 12.20. A double attendance was marked on the instruction of Director of Education. Teachers returned in the afternoon to mark all of the 65 candidates' papers.

31 Jan 1952. Miss C___ is absent.

10.40. Miss C___ is present having arrived late and failed to inform me.

8 Feb 1952. Classes marched to the Cross to hear the proclamation of the accession of Her Majesty Queen Elizabeth.

15 Feb 1952. The late King George VI is being buried today. Older pupils attended a service in the church and a two minute silence was observed.

13 Nov 1952. Telegram received from Mr P. to say that he is absent suffering from a cold.

22 May 1953. Coronation gifts were distributed and school closed for three days Coronation holidays.

25 June 1953. Primary 7 pupils accompanied by the Headmaster and their teachers attended the Royal Highland Show at Alloa.

26 June 1953. All pupils from 7 upwards, accompanied by their teachers attended a showing of the film 'A Queen Is Crowned'.

25 Nov 1953. The Medway hut, which was occupied by classes 3a and 3b has been evacuated because the electric installation and wiring cannot be used for heating and also because of the unsatisfactory flooring. The pupils have gone back to the hall.

16 March 1955. Parents of boys being presented for the Control Exam interviewed today. The majority of parents attended, including many fathers.

17 March 1955. Parents of girls being presented for Control Exam interviewed today.

1 July 1955. Tomorrow the Queen will visit the town and all pupils not parading with Youth Organisations will be assembled in the playground and then conducted to the Cross where they will welcome Her Majesty.

13 March 1956. Miss L, a former teacher, was buried today. School closed at 3 o'clock as a mark of respect.

21 August 56. School re-opened today. Two teachers short. Permission received to recruit two teachers on a temporary basis.

22 Aug 1956, Visiting Art teacher Mr M___ has departed on National Service.

15 Jan 1957. County Architect visited school with a view to providing more classrooms to house increased roll.

13 March 1957. Depute Director of Education visited school to discuss accommodation for extra class at Easter.

24 Feb 1958. Mr F___ has been transferred to secondary because of a shortage of teachers in the Maths Dept.

31 Oct 1958. Hallowe'en Carnival held to raise money for school funds.

12 June 1959. Headmaster out of school today attending Educational Institute of Scotland A.G.M.

19 Jan 1960. Owing to terrible conditions, snow and slush underfoot and to the wet state of the children, the school closed at 12.30, a double attendance was marked.

23 Feb 1960. Circular from Director of Education intimating that Friday will be observed as a holiday to celebrate the birth of a son to the Queen.

22 Aug 1960. School re-opened today. Overcrowding very severe. Classes in halls in all parts of the town.

27 March 1961. Visiting art teacher has been re-timetabled for secondary work.

28 Oct 1961. Mr M retired Headmaster commenced duty today to help relieve staffing position.

22 May 1962. The school won the shield for athletics at the District Sports.

8 Oct 1962. As a result of a tragic motor van accident one of our 8 year old pupils died last night.

30 Nov 1963. Divine service was held for all pupils on this St Andrew's Day.

21 Dec 1963. Two double hutted classrooms erected in playground.

8 Jan 1964. A class in French was started today, formed from most able ten pupils from each of three Qualifying classes.

19 Feb 1964. Problem Arithmetic and Composition for Qualifying Exam were carried out today.

3 July 1964. Miss B___ retired after 43 years service in this school.

7 Oct 1964. Fourteen teachers have signed a letter to the Director indicating that they refuse to carry out supervisory duties in the dining hall.

25 Nov 1964. Very large turnout of parents at open night.

29 June 1965. The Headmaster retires today.

23 Aug 1965. The school opened with an inauguration service for the new Headmaster.

20 May 1966. Parent Teacher Association bring and buy sale held in school hall.

2 June 1966. District Sports shield won for 5th successive time.

22 Aug 1966. Miss H___ absent. Fractured her hip while pony trekking during summer holidays.

16 Aug 1967. New infants were enrolled over two days. This proved a good arrangement.

12 Feb 1969. All pupils involved in school concert.

23 Sept 1970. Staff course on decimalisation and metrication.

14 June 1972. Electricity strike. Power cuts.

12 June 1972. Senior pupils visited exhibition to mark centenary of compulsory education in Scotland.

13 Nov 1972. Showing of police film 'Never Go With Strangers'.

20 Nov 1972. Holiday to mark Silver Wedding of H.M. Queen Elizabeth and H.R.H. Prince Philip, Duke of Edinburgh.

25 Nov 1972. Former Headmaster died today.

5 June 1973. Pupils attended Sadler's Wells Opera Workshop.

9 Oct 1973. Headmaster attended district meeting with new Primary Adviser.

14 Nov 1973. Holiday for wedding of H.R.H. Princess Anne.

3 Dec 1973. Film show for all pupils about Dr Barnardo's Homes.

19 March 1974. Feeder school Heads met Secondary Rector to discuss primary secondary liaison.

10 Oct 1974. School closed for Parliamentary Election.

31 Oct 1974. School closed because of official Educational Institute of Scotland strike about teachers' pay. Five members of staff elected not to strike.

– 15 –
HOMEWORK

Suggestions for places to visit and other books to read

GLASGOW'S SCOTLAND STREET SCHOOL MUSEUM is an excellent starting point for readers who wish to research further into the lives of the dominies.

Edinburgh also has a school museum situated on the top floor of St Mary's Primary School, London Street, but it is designed to serve school classes conducting projects on Scottish education and is not open to the public except on special occasions such as Open Doors Day. The best alternative in the capital is The Museum of Childhood, High Street, on the Royal Mile, which, as well as a schoolroom tableau on the top floor, is particularly strong on playground games and children's out of school pastimes. It also frequently stages special displays on topics such as school books, school holidays etc.

In the Borders an interesting place to visit is the little school room in Biggar's Gladstone Court Museum, where, unlike most other museums, a hands on approach is positively encouraged.

In Fife, Dunfermline's Abbot's House, being close to Lochgelly, has a special exhibit on school straps, including a monster tawse sculpture by George Wyllie, created as a result of a subscription from Beath High School, the secondary school in Cowdenbeath, where John J. Dick's famous saddlery business is now situated. Kirkcaldy Museum also has a small display of artefacts from local schools.

On Tayside, Dundee's McManus Museum has a schoolroom display and The Retreat, the museum run by local volunteers in Glen Esk near Edzell, and the Signal Tower Museum in Arbroath both have school-related exhibits.

In Perthshire and the Highlands the museum in the former Poor House at Grandtully on the road from Dunkeld to Aberfeldy, and the museum at Corgaff on the road from Braemar to Tomintoul, both have education-related exhibits. There are also museums of childhood in Aviemore and Strathpeffer.

Read more about it

THE BOOKS CONSULTED during research for *The Dominie* included *The History of the The Burgh Schools of Scotland* by Grant, *History of Education in Scotland* by Wright, *Scottish School Humour* by Thomson, *School Life in Old Scotland* by Pratt, Travels and *Tales of a School Inspector* by Wilson, and various histories of individual Scottish secondary schools including those of Ayr, Bathgate, Fortrose, Morrisons Academy Crieff, Stirling, Glasgow High School and Hutchesons College, Glasgow, and Daniel Stewarts College, Edinburgh, Melville College, Edinburgh, George Watsons College, Edinburgh, Leith Academy, Royal High School, Edinburgh, St Margaret's School, Edinburgh, Edinburgh Academy, Fettes College, Edinburgh and Loretto School, Musselburgh.

Most of the above are out of print, but may be consulted at The National Library of Scotland, Geroge IV Bridge, Edinburgh.

The Maister

(Anonymous)

He gied us Scriptur' names tae spell,
But what they meant we couldna' tell,
He maybe didna' ken himsel',
The Maister.
What funny dogs we used tae draw,
Upon oor slates, an ships an' a',
Till keekin' roond wi' fright we saw,
The Maister.
He gie'd oor lugs a fearful pu',
Said he wad skelp us black and blue,
I doot he wouldna try that noo,
The Maister.
We mind them weel
his lang black taws,
They nippit sair like partan claws,
A crabbit little man he was,
The Maister.
He opened aye the schule wi prayer,
An' psalms an' questions gied us mair
than what we thocht was proper there —
The Maister.
An' after time an' siller spent,
We left as wise as when we went,
It wisnae muckle that he kent —
The Maister.
It's forty years noo since that day,
An' time, whose besom's aye at play,
Like many other things has swept away —
The Maister.